The Real Bogie
and Bacall

For the whole family on the sofa,
with love.

The Real Bogie and Bacall

Catherine Curzon

WHITE OWL

AN IMPRINT OF PEN & SWORD BOOKS LTD
YORKSHIRE – PHILADELPHIA

First published in Great Britain in 2024 by
WHITE OWL
an imprint of Pen & Sword Books Ltd
Yorkshire – Philadelphia

Typeset by Concept, Huddersfield, West Yorkshire, HD4 5JL.
Printed and bound in England by CPI Group (UK) Ltd, Croydon, CR0 4YY.

Pen & Sword Books Ltd incorporates the imprints of Aviation, Atlas, Family
History, Fiction, Maritime, Military, Discovery, Politics, History, Archaeology,
Select, Wharncliffe Local History, Wharncliffe True Crime, Military Classics,
Wharncliffe Transport, Leo Cooper, The Praetorian Press, Remember When,
White Owl, Seaforth Publishing and Frontline Books.

For a complete list of Pen & Sword titles please contact
PEN & SWORD BOOKS LTD
47 Church Street, Barnsley, South Yorkshire, S70 2AS, England
E-mail: enquiries@pen-and-sword.co.uk
Website: www.pen-and-sword.co.uk
or
PEN & SWORD BOOKS
1950 Lawrence Rd, Havertown, PA 19083, USA
E-mail: uspen-and-sword@casematepublishers.com
Website: www.penandswordbooks.com

Contents

Act Three: Bogie and Baby

Acknowledgements

The warmest thanks go to Jon, not only the man who has given me opportunity after opportunity and made this possible, but also the sort of friend one doesn't find too often, and all the team at Pen & Sword. Much love and cuppas are always due to K, R, and H, for football talk, listing nonsense and all those worlds.

Mr C and Pippa, you're my world, and always will be.

Introduction

Slim: This is about the time for it, isn't it?
Steve: The time for what?
Slim: The story of my life. How do you want me to begin?

This book is the product of a lifetime in black and white. More than four decades after I was first dazzled by its lustre, the Golden Age of Hollywood still glitters for me, and Bogie and Bacall's love story might've come straight from the big screen.

Legendary couples in Hollywood are not difficult to find. Rhett and Scarlett, Robin and Marion, even Lady and the Tramp have become some of the most celebrated pairings of the Golden Age of movies. Ask anyone to name a Hollywood couple and it's a fair chance that they'll choose at least one immortalised in fiction, but Tinseltown's most iconic duo were as real as it gets. Humphrey Bogart and Lauren Bacall were never meant to fall in love, and nobody who knew them would have expected it. When they met, he was already a superstar and she was a nobody. Thrice married and middle-aged, on screen Bogie was a tough guy par excellence, and his reputation off screen was that of a hard-living drunk. Lauren Bacall was twenty-five years his junior, a model with precious little acting experience and even less profile. Yet when the cameras rolled, sparks flew. Their love story was one that wouldn't have been out of place on the silver screen, and it's an honour to tell it.

I first encountered Bogie and Bacall on a wet, grey winter afternoon in the tiny village where my grandparents lived. It was as far from Hollywood as could be, but it was a place where the Golden Age had never ended. Some of my earliest memories are sitting before the blazing coal fire in that little sitting room, eyes wide at the glamorous gals and hard-bitten men, terrified of Karloff's creature or crying with laughter at Buster Keaton. I've always credited my grandad with my love of telling stories, but I should credit him with my love of film too – I was crazy about the Rat Pack long before I had heard of the Brat Pack of my 1980s childhood.

This book isn't an exhaustive examination of the films of Bogie and Bacall, but it is a labour of love that began back in that little cottage. Today, the fire I sit in front of is my own and my beloved grandfather is no longer here, but the love of classic Hollywood that he instilled in me shines as bright as ever. That's why it's such a privilege to tell the story of Bogie and Bacall, one that burns with more passion than anything Hollywood could've imagined in its wildest dreams. After all, who doesn't love a love story?

Act One

Bogart

'Whatever you do, never, never let 'em find out how easy it all is.'[1]

Belmont and Maud

Bogart's screen presence is one for the ages, and his persona was crafted over a lifetime. Hard-bitten, cynical and whip smart, to his fans he never looked like he was acting. He seemed born to the shadows of noir and the trench coat and fedora, made to sip Scotch in a smoky bar. Yet Bogie's beginnings belie the instinctual ease with which he became Queeg and Sam Spade, or Marlowe and Rick Blaine, for this was no child of a Hell's Kitchen tenement or a Bronx walk-up.

Humphrey DeForest Bogart was the eldest child of Belmont DeForest Bogart and Maud Humphrey. They were a wealthy and accomplished couple who were as far from the mean streets as could be. Mrs Bogart was a commercial illustrator who made her firstborn her model in the cradle, whilst her husband was a doctor who had graduated from Columbia before going on to receive a medical degree from Yale. Dr Bogart romanced the family history into one of trailblazers and ground shakers, reimagining his hard-working Dutch immigrant ancestors as prominent early settlers in New York, but Maud Humphrey had no need to make up stories.

Maud's ancestors had come to America on the *Mayflower* and she had grown up in a wealthy enclave of Rochester, New York, where she showed an early and prodigious artistic talent. In her early 20s, Lady Maud, as she became known, travelled to Paris to further her training under James McNeill Whistler. She returned to the US ready to take the world of illustration by storm.

Whilst Belmont was focused on a future in cardiac surgery, Maud became one of the most in-demand artists in the city. She specialised in playful illustrations of children – the Humphrey Baby – and commercial portraits that captured all the hope and promise of the new century. Her work was bright, attractive and aspirational, and it was snapped up by

1

some of America's most famous brands. As Maud's professional achievements soared, she became as familiar on the Manhattan social scene as her work had become across America.

When Belmont and Maud met at a party in New York, they seemed like the perfect match. Belmont made $20,000 per year but Maud, flying high as the most famous illustrative artist of the day, was easily banking more than double that. It wasn't only the couple's financial disparity that challenged the status quo either. Unsurprisingly for a modern gal, Maud was passionate about woman's suffrage, and that passion eventually ended her fledgling romance with the doctor. Though only one year divided them, Belmont was a product of a different age and Maud had fully embraced the future. Maud couldn't and wouldn't conform to the blueprint of a subservient nineteenth-century woman that Belmont wanted.

In 1898, Belmont suffered an accident that changed not only his life, but the future of cinema. Whilst he was riding in an ambulance, the horse pulling the vehicle spooked and it overturned. Belmont suffered a badly broken leg that was exacerbated when initial efforts to set it caused further damage. The couple reconciled during a sentimental visit Maud made to Belmont's hospital bedside, the very place where they were married that summer.

The Bogarts made their home alongside a small household staff at 245 West 103rd Street, a fashionable address for a fashionable couple. Maud worked out of her home studio whilst Belmont continued his glittering medical career, and neither had much interest in Manhattan's social calendar. 'She was essentially a woman who loved work, loved her work, to the exclusion of everything else,' was Bogie's recollection in a 1949 article tellingly entitled 'I Can't Say I Loved Her'. 'She was totally incapable of showing affection. Her caress was a kind of blow. She clapped you on a shoulder, almost the way a man does.'[2] As the years passed, that never changed. Maud was devoted to her work and Belmont to his patients until both turned their affections to morphine; there was little warmth from either.

The Humphrey Baby

Humphrey DeForest Bogart was born in Sloan's Maternity Hospital, Manhattan, on 25 December 1899. He was given his mother's maiden name and was the most welcome Christmas gift his parents could've wished for. Bogie himself was a little more pragmatic, later telling friends and family that his Christmas Day arrival left him 'gypped out of a proper birthday, goddammit'.[3] From the moment he made his first appearance, it seemed as though the path of the little boy's life was already set. Belmont put his son's name down for his old prep school, Phillips Andover, and looked forward to the day that Humphrey would follow him to Columbia and Yale then into a medical career of his own. Maud, meanwhile, gave him an early start in entertainment, and her illustrations made him famous across the country as the face of the Mellin's Baby Food Company. It was a far cry from film noir.

The family was completed by two daughters, Frances and Catherine, known as Pat and Kay respectively, but it was Bogie that caused Maud the most concern. Though he survived a bout of childhood pneumonia, it left his mother permanently nervous about his delicate health. 'He is a manly lad, but too delicate for rougher games,'[4] Maud lamented, deciding instead that her son was better suited to life as her model rather than roughhousing with his friends. It was a rare glimpse of concern from the woman who liked to keep things strictly business, even her family ties.

As the little family grew and the Bogarts tussled for control, it was Maud's progressive way that won the day. The children called her by her first name, though Belmont was always 'Father', and just as Belmont had little Humphrey's life all mapped out, Maud did likewise for her daughters. Unfortunately, her vision of her girls as independent women was at odds with Belmont's ambitions for them to become society wives. In the Bogart household, such fundamental disagreements were common-place as traditional values clashed against progressive ambitions time and time again.

Maud and Belmont had already gone their separate ways once thanks to their different outlooks on life, but they were married now: splitting up again wasn't something to be undertaken lightly. Instead they kept up the façade of a respectable and successful family, whilst behind the scenes life became more and more miserable. The Bogarts were at war. 'We kids would pull the covers around our ears to keep out the sound of fighting,' Bogie remembered, under no illusions that it was keeping up appearances rather than love that held the family together. 'We were not an affectionate family,' he confessed as he approached his fiftieth birthday. 'It was difficult for us to kiss.'[5]

Nor could the youngsters have missed Belmont's increasing reliance on morphine, which he had first used in the aftermath of his accident, nor the debilitating migraines that frayed Maud's temper. Bogie recalled that his upbringing had been a world away from the idyllic portraits his mother produced to such acclaim, with affection in short supply. A kiss or an embrace was an event in the Bogart household and the children were raised in the most part by servants who came and went at a rate of knots, chased away by Maud and Belmont's unpredictable moods. Little wonder that Bogie admitted pragmatically that Maud had his respect and admiration, but never his love. Had he sent her flowers and a loving message to celebrate Mother's Day, Bogie reflected in adulthood, 'she would have returned the wire and flowers to me, collect'.[6]

And when they weren't arguing, Maud and Belmont were working; he in his consulting rooms on the ground floor of their Manhattan home, she in her studio at the top of the house. Even at school Bogie couldn't catch a break. His friends made him the target of relentless teasing, mocking him for the fame he'd achieved as the chubby-cheeked, curly-haired Humphrey Baby. Ever defiant of convention, Bogie attempted to cultivate a more masculine image and outdoorsy lifestyle, but Maud's decision to dress him as Little Lord Fauntleroy and teach him to dance didn't help. She was sowing the seeds of a lifelong rebellion.

The Seneca Point Gang

The Bogart children sought an escape from the realities of domestic warfare in their own worlds. When the family took up summer residence at a vast estate named Willow Brook on the shores of Canandaigua Lake, young Humphrey was inducted into his father's love of boating. For the rest of his life, whenever things got too much, he fled for the open water.

In the bucolic idyll of Willow Brook, Bogie finally found some respite from his parents' squabbles and even became the leader of a gang of local lads, who called themselves – without too much inspiration – the Seneca Point Gang. They nicknamed Humphrey 'Hump' and it was he who dictated how days would be spent. Hump was also the director behind the little plays that the gang put on for an audience that had paid a nickel each to watch young Bogie at work. He found inspiration in silent movie theatres and vaudeville houses, where for a few cents a boy could buy a world of entertainment and an escape from the fights that raged at home. By the time the Bogarts sold the 55-acre rural retreat and purchased a summer home on Fire Island in 1915, life at Willow Brook had already left an indelible impact on Bogie.

If Bogie's characters seemed to have been dragged up on the streets of New York City and finished at the University of Life, the reality couldn't have been more different. Bogie enjoyed the sort of education that only the wealthy could afford, attending first the Delancey School before moving on to Trinity School. Having spent too long trussed up as Little Lord Fauntleroy, young Hump loathed the formal uniforms of blue Eton suits with their matching waistcoats, and accessorised his with a fashionable derby. He was never happy in academia and ill health plagued his school career. Scarlet fever forced him to repeat a year and by the time Bogie was enrolled in Phillips Andover, where Belmont had flourished, he had lost what little interest he ever had in formal education.

Phillips wasn't the sort of place that encouraged its pupils to express themselves too freely. It was a traditional school for traditional families, but young Hump wasn't a traditional boy. In New York, Bogie had been kept apart from his schoolmates by his mother, who preferred her son to come straight home at the end of the day and pose for her illustrations, but now he would board in Massachusetts for the final year of his school life. Belmont still hoped that his son might follow him to Yale, but that particular ship had long since sailed.

Bogie didn't know what he wanted to do, but he knew that he didn't want to bury his nose in books. He didn't last long at Phillips. His short time there ended in expulsion, not because he dunked a teacher in the duckpond or smashed the headmaster's window, as Bogie and his fellow pupils would later claim, but because of failing grades and a preference for booze and girls over the classroom. He was bewitched by a freckled girl named Pickles and another named Bonnie, and they proved to be so much fun that studying was soon way down on Bogie's list of priorities.

'The bastards threw me out,' Bogie complained as he packed his bags, but he remained fond of Phillips Andover despite his ignominious departure. It was the place where he had finally escaped from Maud's long shadow; he had no intention of falling under it again.

Bogie returned to New York to find his parents united at last. The only trouble was, what had brought them together was shared anger at his expulsion and a mutual belief that their son lacked direction. A furious Belmont told Bogie that he would spend the war working as a naval architect in a New York shipyard, but Hump had other ideas. If he was going to do his bit, it wouldn't be in Manhattan.

The Story of a Scar

'What does death mean to a kid of seventeen? The idea of death starts getting through to you only when you're older,'[7] Bogie reflected as he

5

looked back on the decision he made when he headed home from Massachusetts. Keen to offer more than he could in a New York shipyard, Bogie enlisted in the Navy. And a little bit of the Bogart myth was born.

Humphrey Bogart's stiff upper lip and characteristic lisp were two of the most recognisable things about him, central to his hard-bitten persona and every bad Bogie impression that has ever existed. How he acquired that scarred lip and the attendant lisp is one of the great mysteries of Hollywood, and there have been more than a few explanations over the years.

Bogie's sister, Pat, remembered that Belmont's hot temper had got the better of him and he had smacked Bogie in the mouth, leaving him with permanent nerve damage. When Belmont was done, Maud told him that if he laid a hand on the children again, it'd be the last thing he ever did. As an adult, meanwhile, Bogie confided to actor David Niven that the scar had been the result of an innocent childhood accident. He blamed the doctor who treated him for the subsequent nerve damage and complained, 'instead of stitching it up, he screwed it up'.[8] Perhaps that unnamed physician was his own father. Later the story received an added coda in which Belmont bodged an attempt at corrective surgery, making things even worse.

Bogie remembered things very differently. Either he or the studio – David Niven certainly thought it was down to the Hollywood publicity machine – preferred a version of events more befitting of a movie star. In this telling, Bogie suffered an injury when *Leviathan*, the ship on which he was serving, was shelled, and a splinter of wooden shrapnel pierced his lip. This seems unlikely, since he didn't join the crew of Leviathan until the war had ended, but Hollywood never let the truth get in the way of a good story.

Another even more dramatic version of events was put forward by Bogie's friends, who remembered a story about him escorting a prisoner to Portsmouth Naval Prison in New Hampshire. The compliant prisoner's hands were manacled together but when he asked Bogie for a cigarette, he was happy to comply. As Bogie was about to light the cigarette, the prisoner slammed the manacles into his face and took off running.

Bleeding from a wound in his lip, Bogie was able to bring down the fleeing prisoner by shooting him in the leg. When he eventually sought treatment for his injury, the Portsmouth doctor did a poor job and the resultant scar caused Bogie's characteristic lisp. Of all three versions, this one seems the most likely, and it's certainly the story that Bogie's friends believed. Though a beating from Belmont might play into the myth of a disaffected young man trapped in a home filled with conflict, and the story of the shrapnel splinter has all the hallmarks of Hollywood, a smack in the mouth from a desperate man has a ring of truth to it. Perhaps the idea of Bogie cheerfully giving his prisoner a cigarette wasn't in keeping with his tough guy image – the idea of a beating from his father certainly wasn't – but in all other respects it fits with young Bogie's nature. Somewhat sheltered, raised in cotton wool and trusting on one hand, but able to drop a fleeing prisoner with a bullet on the other, it's somehow strangely appropriate.

Bogie was given an honourable discharge in 1919 and returned home to New York once more. Now he seemed to belong there less than ever, a stranger in that genteel home in that genteel neighbourhood, where things never changed. Yet something had changed, and Belmont's long reliance on morphine had finally begun to take a toll. Addled by narcotics and badly advised by friends, he had made a series of bad investments that squandered the family fortune. Many of Belmont's wealthiest patients deserted him and he was reduced to working as a doctor on board ocean liners. Bogie returned home not to a hero's welcome or even an embrace but to Maud's cool, 'Good job, Bogie.' It was hardly the stuff of the movies.

In New York, Bogie now faced the same problem as so many returning veterans: what would he do with the rest of his life? With no qualifications and precious few prospects, Belmont's connections came good at last and Bogie embarked on a string of going-nowhere jobs, but the war had awakened an ambition that had until now seemed absent. New York had plenty to keep a young man busy, but as Bogie watched his friends from the Seneca Point Gang make strides in their personal and professional lives, he wondered when his moment would come.

Footlights

In the end, Bogie's big break came out of nowhere. Since the days of the Seneca Point Gang, one of Bogie's best friends had been Bill Brady Jr, the son of Bill Brady Sr, an impresario whose productions provided costumes for the boys' amateur theatricals. Brady had made a fortune in the movies, so when Bill Jr asked if he could set Bogie up with a job – it didn't matter how lowly – Bill Sr took him on as an office runner. It was the start of a new life for Bogie and he climbed the ranks swiftly, eventually finding himself standing in as director when a movie called *Life* lost its original helmer. It soon lost Bogie too, as he was swiftly removed from the seat of power once Brady realised just how bad a director he made. A foray into writing similarly ended in disappointment and with each knock, Bogie became more and more certain that he was on the road to dismissal.

Bill Jr went in to bat for his old friend and convinced his actress step-mother, Grace George, to give Bogie the dual job of stage manager and male understudy on the 1921 tour of *The Ruined Lady*. Bogie never expected to go on, but when the juvenile lead fell ill he was called on to perform. His one and only rehearsal was a disaster. 'I took one look at the emptiness where the audience would be,' Bogie remembered, 'And I couldn't remember anything.'[9] Grace took pity on her co-star and charitably came down with a sore throat that cancelled the performance. Bogie's planned debut was over before it began.

Bogie's big moment eventually came with the forgotten 1922 play, *Drifting*, where H. D. Bogart was cast alongside Helen Menken, destined to become the first Mrs Humphrey Bogart. She was brought in at the last minute when the leading lady went into labour, and had just one night to learn the part. Helen's first performance was a nightmare and though she soldiered bravely on amid falling scenery and misplaced blocking, her nerves were shattered. Furious at herself and the world in general, after the curtain fell she turned on Bogie and bellowed at him. 'I booted her,' Bogie recalled, with just a hint of shame. 'She, in turn, belted me and ran to her dressing room to cry.'[10] It was an inauspicious start, but the strong-willed, fiery Helen was everything Bogie loved in a woman. Within days they were a couple and within weeks they had a marriage licence, but it would take four more years before they finally tied the knot.

Bogie made little impact in *Drifting*, but Brady was happy to keep booking him whenever he had gaps to plug in a cast. This was no *42nd Street* moment, but a Wild West sort of Broadway, where plays were opening and closing all the time and though Bogie might not be leading man material, he knew how to deliver a line. Sort of. And even if he couldn't, as a minor cog in a large cast, it wasn't as if anyone would notice the occasional fluffed line.

Yet for a hard-bitten producer, Bill Brady Sr had a weak spot for his friends. Aware that things hadn't been going so well for the Bogarts, when Belmont asked if there was any possibility that he could find a bigger role for Bogie, Bill decided to take a chance. He cast Bogie as a seductive libertine in *Swifty* and made it his business to turn the young man into something resembling an actor. From his seat in the gods, Brady subjected

Bogie to a baptism of fire, barking directions at him and yelling 'What?' every time a line was inaudible. The rehearsal process was brutal, but it worked. He, more than anybody, might be said to have kneaded the raw dough of Humphrey Bogart, but it was to no avail. *Swifty* was a bomb, and nobody bombed bigger than Bogie, who was dismissed by critic Alexander Woollcott in a review that Maud read aloud over breakfast.

'The young man who embodied the aforesaid sprig,' wrote Woollcott, 'was what might mercifully be described as inadequate.'[11] Bogie was stung; he clipped out the review and kept it for the rest of his life. He was determined that he would never be called inadequate again. Quite by accident, that critic had ignited a fire under him that would not go out.

Some actors need to act. It's like oxygen, or a mask they don to protect the person within, or even to provide them with a sense of identity that they believe they otherwise lack. Bogie wasn't one of them. What he needed was a purpose, some way to tie up the dangling threads of what seemed like an aimless life once and for all. His had been a confused and confusing existence and his first two decades left him feeling rudderless. On the one hand Maud and Belmont had been undemonstrative parents, not given to expressions of affection and absent either physically or emotionally. On the other hand, young Bogie had been dressed up like a Gainsborough portrait and spirited away from his school at the end of each day to sit for portraits. Whenever an opportunity arose for social or sporting events where he might have made friends, a maid in a starched uniform whisked him back to Maud's airless studio. He had been shuttled from one expensive school to the next, each more focused than the last on carving young Hump into a gentleman and a scholar, but with every new school or each new dance step, he was quietly brooding on rebellion. Little wonder that Bogie loved the solitude he found out on the lake, or the carefree fun of the gang's amateur theatricals. When he was caught shooting out the lights on his school playing fields, it was the act of a child who was trying to play the tough guy. That would one day be Bogie's greatest role.

Life in Brady's dramatic company gave Bogie something to do, but he didn't dream of the limelight. He fell into Brady's company by accident and ended up on stage simply because there was a vacancy. Yet for all his streetwise play-acting, Bogie's schooling and upper-middle-class roots oozed from his pores, and he knew it. But as the Depression bit down and the fortunes of the family plummeted along with those of America, Bogie worked to keep hold of his fledgling career. If he lost it now, it might be gone forever.

Wet Pants Willies

In these early years, Bogie was a familiar figure on the Manhattan party scene, usually with a different girl on his arm every night. Prohibition was no barrier for those who knew where to lay their hands on booze and Bogie and his friends certainly did. His love of partying almost killed his career before it had taken off, when Brady entrusted him with a major role in a 1923 production of *Meet the Wife* opposite Mary Boland and Clifton Webb. In this light farce, *Variety* picked Bogie out as 'clean-looking juvenile [who] made a pleasant lover'.[12] The praise might not be over-whelming, but it beat inadequate. *The Billboard* went a little further, and Bogie could finally add a more positive review to his scrapbook: 'One of the most promising members of the younger generation of actors. He is of the dark and romantic type, lending the requisite touch of youth to "Meet the Wife".'[13]

Meet the Wife ran for more than 200 performances, but Bogie was already growing tired of what he called 'Wet Pants Willie' roles. There was no longevity for the flannel-clad ingenue who bounded onto the stage with a tennis racket and asked brightly, 'Tennis, anyone?' Years later, in a very different sort of role, Bogie's definitive Philip Marlowe would get the last word on Wet Pants Willies and their pesky love of tennis. There would be no room in *The Big Sleep* for a flannel-clad ingenue.

Vivian: My, you're a mess, aren't you?
Marlowe: I'm not very tall either. Next time I'll come on stilts, wear a white tie and carry a tennis racket.
Vivian: I doubt if even that would help.

Yet Philip Marlowe was still a couple of decades in the future, and Bogie was looking no further ahead than his next paycheque. He had a hit, and he needed to capitalise on it. In the same 1924 edition of *The Billboard* that sang his praises, a breathless puff-piece on the young actor played up his sterling efforts to step in and save *The Ruined Lady* when its juvenile lead fell ill. The write-up isn't too remarkable, other than the fact that it offers an early glimpse at the kind of press attention that would eventually become Bogie's bread and butter. Readers were told of his poise, his 'manly stage presence' and even his baritone, 'neglected because its possessor has been either too busy or too broke to give attention to its cultivation'.[14] The piece isn't without a pensive word from the actor himself either, with Bogie ruminating on the true nature of greatness. For a man who became a legend, Bogie's humility never deserted him.

'No one was ever born to be great,' he said with the wisdom of youth, and he believed it. 'They become great thru concentrated effort. The failure of many born with talent proves that talent without effort is wasted.'[15]

Meet the Wife was Bogie's chance to make a mark in one of Brady's premier productions, and he was in a celebratory mood. Each night, when the curtain fell, Bogie and his newest squeeze went out and partied, safe in the knowledge that he'd have the whole day to sleep it off. Perhaps inevitably, the drinking sessions got longer and the hangovers got worse until Bogie was good as a zombie on stage. Things came to a head when, instead of delivering Mary Boland's cue, he slumped in a boozy daze against the set, breathing alcohol fumes all over his leading lady. Boland had no choice but to style it out, desperately improvising until her co-star remembered his line. That night, when the curtain fell, Boland shredded Bogie. She told him that she would never work with him again.

Once again, Bogie seemed to have put his foot in it. But this time, rather than double down or throw in the towel, he took the embarrassing incident as a lesson well learned. From that day on, Humphrey Bogart made a vow that he would approach his career as a professional. He would nurture it, not drink it away.

Helen

As Bogie was ruminating on the nature of greatness in *The Billboard*, right across the page was a casting notice for *Nerves*, which would bring him good reviews in an admittedly small part. It seemed as though he would be toiling to achieve greatness forever. *Nerves* saw Bogie take his first steps into drama, as one of three idealistic young friends who confront the horrors of war head on. Also among the cast was Mary Philips, the future second Mrs Bogart, and she made an immediate impact as she sashayed away across the stage, stealing the attention of the audience from what should have been Bogie's big moment. After the performance, he read her the riot act, but Mary simply gave a smouldering smile. '"Suppose you try to stop me," she challenged,' Bogie reminisced. 'Well, I didn't try to stop her because while I was talking to her I suddenly became aware that here was a girl with whom I could very easily fall in love.'[16] The flirtation was on.

11

Mary's charms played second fiddle to Bogie's excellent notices for *Nerves*. Perhaps most important of all were the laurels bestowed on him by critic Alexander Woollcott, who had once branded Bogie 'inadequate', a verdict that had cut deep. 'Mr Bogart is a young actor whose appearance was recorded by your correspondent in words so disparaging that it is surprising to find him still acting,' wrote Woollcott in his review of *Nerves*. 'Those words are hereby eaten.'[17] Unfortunately, though the critics applauded *Nerves*, it failed to ignite the box office and closing notices were posted after less than a month.

There was something more than professional pride behind Bogie's determination to succeed. Helen Menken, already a stage veteran when Bogie fell for her in 1922, enjoyed a considerable reputation both on Broadway and the touring circuit alike. Her salary reflected her star status and for Bogie, just like Belmont before him, that was a sticking point. He had grown up in a household with a female breadwinner and as far as he was concerned, that had played a significant part in the Bogarts' troubled marriage. The desire to become Helen's professional equal gave him the push he needed to attack every role with relish, earning longer and more lucrative engagements with each passing season. Those once brutal reviews now glowed, but every time Bogie thought about wedding bells, Helen's career reached another milestone and he shied away again.

Helen's professional achievements brought with them a new raft of problems. As an up-and-coming young actor who was gathering good notices, Bogart could only benefit professionally from marriage to Helen Menken, who counted some of the most influential names in New York theatre amongst her best friends. Bogie talked the matter over with his buddies, confiding in Bill Brady Jr that it wasn't a question of not wanting to marry Helen – he just wasn't sure that he wanted to get married full stop. Brady reminded him of the cold reality of his romance with one of the most popular divas on Broadway: if Bogart won her heart, the future could be bright. If he broke it, he'd be thrown to the wolves.

Bogart loved Helen in his way, in so far as he knew how at that point in his life, but his views on marriage had been tarnished by his parents' relationship. Instead of making things legal, the couple decided to live together, an arrangement that soon proved to be at odds with Bogie's upper-middle-class upbringing in genteel Manhattan. Though he disingenuously told his friends that Helen bullied him into marriage, the truth was that Bogie's rakish partying and louche lifestyle were no match for Belmont's patrician genes. Bogie simply had to do the decent thing. So, in

May 1926, the couple were married in Helen Menken's Gramercy Park Hotel apartment.

From the start, the omens were terrible. Helen's mother and father were both deaf and communicated in sign language. It was understandably important to Helen that they feel included in the ceremony, and a deaf minister was chosen to officiate. The wedding was to be conducted in sign language whilst the minister spoke the words aloud to a congregation that included some of Broadway's brightest leading lights. When the minister began to speak, it was in an unexpected falsetto that raised a few eyebrows and titters. All too aware of the phalanx of society reporters who were present to cover her wedding, Helen became increasingly hysterical. Eventually she fled the room and had to be convinced to return to her nuptials.

Bogie had already doubted the wisdom of marriage and, within weeks, he was convinced that he should have listened to his gut. He was approaching 30 and wanted something more traditional than throwaway romances or marriage to a career gal could offer. Bogie, who had never known a nurturing home, wanted someone to look after him. He envisioned a pliant housewife who would be waiting when he got home – no matter how late or how drunk – and that wasn't Helen.

Helen was living the life of a Broadway diva and loving it. When she came home from the theatre each evening, she enjoyed a standing ovation in the lobby of the Gramercy Park and her dog dined on caviar rather than hamburger meat. Bogie couldn't accept it, but he wouldn't back down. Each disagreement grew into a battle royal that inevitably ended with husband or wife storming out in a fury. Bogie had always feared a marriage that turned out like Maud and Belmont's and in his union to Helen Menken, that was exactly what he got. Within six months of their wedding, the couple had already undergone several short separations, yet as 1926 drew to a close, Helen was determined to give it her all. She had recently ended a long and incredibly successful theatrical engagement but just as she found herself with some time to devote to Bogie, he was opening in Roscoe 'Fatty' Arbuckle's short-lived comeback show. Hot on its heels came a leading role in *Saturday's Children*. There was just one hitch: the show was in Chicago.

Though Bogie asked Helen to accompany him on the road, she decided to stay in New York rather than risk missing out on her next big role. That summer, with Bogie still in the States, Helen travelled to England to make her debut in London's West End. When the British press trumpeted that

'The woman who shocked America [a reference to a controversial play she had appeared in] has arrived in London,'[18] there was no mention of the husband to whom she had been married for such a brief time. It was effectively the end of the road for the short-lived Bogart–Menken union. Helen was happy to let the *Daily Mail* know exactly who was to blame.

'I tried to make my marriage the paramount interest of my life,' she told journalists. 'When I married [Bogie] 18 months ago my career was a success, but I was willing to give it up and concentrate my interest on a home.'[19] Yet Bogie had other ideas, according to Miss Menken, and she found herself second best to his stage career, a slight that drove her to London and the friendly journalists she found there. In a short column subtitled 'Helen Menken Says Husband, Also of Stage, Shuns Domesticity', the *Evening Star* broke the news that it was over. 'Bogart, appearing here in "Saturday's Children," regarded his career as of more importance than marital happiness, Miss Menken avers in the bill signed yesterday in the lawyer's office. Neglect and abuse were also charged.'[20]

The couple filed for divorce and Helen pointed the finger of blame at Bogie, whom she claimed had been too obsessed with his career to be a decent husband. The divorce was finalised on 18 November 1927.

Later, Bogie admitted to Lauren Bacall that he believed he was responsible for the breakdown of the marriage. Just to confuse matters, Helen also claimed responsibility for the divorce when speaking to Bacall. It is likely that neither Helen nor Bogie was truly to blame for the catastrophe of their marriage; it had simply been a mistake, a love affair that didn't need to be legally recognised. Both bride and groom were focused on their careers, Helen on preserving her success, Bogie on becoming at least her equal. It was a miserable foundation on which to start a life together, and Bogie's prosaic attitude towards the divorce was shown in a letter to his agent, in which the only concern he showed was for his professional reputation. 'When the whole thing is over Helen and I will be good friends,' he assured his friend Lyman Brown. 'She's a wonderful girl.'[21]

Though Bogie can hardly be accused of having rushed into marriage with Helen, one thing that can be certain is that he learned nothing from it. In keeping with his young actor about town lifestyle, he was soon looking for the next girl. Bogie's only concession was to swear off actresses, determined instead to stick to women who never went near a stage. He didn't want a career woman, but a wife. She would keep house, look after her husband and never receive a standing ovation in a hotel foyer.

Mary

The plans Humphrey Bogart nurtured for his future didn't quite go as he anticipated. For a short time – a very short time – he plunged back into the Manhattan dating scene, but Mary Philips and her sashay had made an impact. Bogie was single again, Mary had no one on her arm – or so her would-be Casanova believed – and her walk, the quintessential sexy wiggle so beloved of starlets, had given Bogie a lot to think about. There was something else that Mary had too: a profile. Just like Helen Menken, Mary Philips had enjoyed a long career on Broadway and would be the perfect other half of an up-and-coming power couple. He had learned nothing.

Not long after Bogie became a free agent he bumped into Mary at a screening of *The Jazz Singer*. For all his hard-bitten image, Bogie was more romantic than playboy and Mary utterly enchanted him. What he didn't know was that Kenneth MacKenna, his *Nerves* co-star, was already squiring her around town. As soon as Bogie discovered that he had a rival, he was determined to prevail. He knew how to woo a woman and he turned his skills to a devastating advantage, leaving MacKenna in the dust. Mary remembered Bogie later for his winning combination of class and old-time charm, but if Bogie had won the battle, he didn't win the war. When the Bogart–Philips marriage inevitably failed, Mary ran back to MacKenna; their subsequent happy marriage saw out the remaining twenty-four years of MacKenna's life.

But for now, Mary's heart belonged to Humphrey Bogart, and both believed they had found the One. Bogie and Mary were wed in her mother's Connecticut apartment on 3 April 1928 and this time it looked as though the marriage might actually work out. The couple seemed well-suited and were a regular fixture on Broadway's social scene, where they partied hard, matching one another drink for drink. Mary was enjoying more success but Bogie was snapping at her professional heels; for a producer they were the golden ticket.

In January 1929, Bogart and Philips appeared together in *The Skyrocket* as a wide-eyed couple who are almost torn apart by money. Though some critics enjoyed the performances, the reviews were far from universally glowing. The Bogart–Philips dream team had stumbled right out of the gate. As 'colourless, uninspiring characters', Variety dismissed the two-some as 'miscast: neither effective in their attempts'. It can have been little comfort to the pair that the play fared no better, 'Basically, the show needs a new play. As it will not live to see a change in weather.'[22]

And in America, the weather was changing for the worse. The Wall Street crash sent a shockwave through the industry that the Bogarts relied on, not to mention the fabric of their own lives. With Broadway backers losing thousands in the crash, curtains fell and the theatres went dark. Collapsing alongside them was the Manhattan nightlife that Broadway had supported. Bars, nightclubs and restaurants were shuttered. Across America, unemployment and poverty soared and on the Great White Way, things were dire.

Depression

As the entertainment industry capsized, Bogie was fortunate enough to be appearing in a hit production of *It's a Wise Child*, but the run was limited and he was desperately looking for his next gig. For Mary, the reality was very different. She had a prominent role in a successful play, something that every actor would've killed for as the Depression deepened. With *It's a Wise Child* fast approaching its final curtain, Bogie was faced with the thing he dreaded most: a wife who was earning whilst he was not.

But Bogart had set out to be successful, so as the American economy crumbled, he turned his sights on a new horizon. His sister Pat was married to Stuart Rose, a story editor for the Fox Film Corporation, and she encouraged her husband to help her brother out. Rose told Bogie that the studio was pursuing a new casting strategy, eschewing established stars in favour of newcomers. The reason behind it was financial rather than artistic: Fox could get lesser-known names on the cheap and nurture them into the next generation of stars. Rose suggested that Bogie come out west and try his luck; after all, there was hardly a stack of work to be had in New York. At first studio executives were reluctant to test Bogie, as they had more than enough handsome young men who could bound across the screen with a tennis racket and a winning smile, but he proved to be as tenacious as ever.

Eventually Humphrey Bogart's name was added to the long list of stage actors to be tested for a part in a film entitled *The Man Who Came Back*. Ultimately the roles went to established names after all, but Bogie's test made an impact. He was offered a contract on an impressive salary of $750 per week, with all his relocation costs covered. It was more money than he had ever earned in his life and Bogie was understandably tempted, but his success meant a difficult decision for Mary. She was riding high on Broadway and to give that up to travel west as Mrs Bogart would mean an end to that all-too-rare success. Ultimately the couple came to a stalemate.

The Bogarts parted ways, with Mary remaining in New York whilst her husband headed out to California.

For the moment, nobody was talking about divorce, but it was agreed that things would have to change. Mary and Bogie decided to pursue an open marriage; essentially, both would be free to see other people, though they would remain married. It wasn't Bogie's natural state.

Bogie arrived in Hollywood still hoping for that lead role in *The Man Who Came Back*, unaware that the part had already gone to established star Charles Farrell. Bogie would earn his $750 a week not in front of the camera, but behind it. Instead of acting, he was employed as a vocal coach to Farrell, whose glittering silent career had stalled since the coming of sound. Bogie hated the job, understandably wondering why he – a supposed unknown – was teaching a headliner how to speak on camera. But even though all of the years of expensive schooling might not have left Bogie with any qualifications, they'd certainly taught him something about diction, and he in turn imparted what he knew to Farrell.

By way of recognition for his sterling coaching work, Bogie was thrown a couple of minor roles as crumbs from the top table. One of these, 1930's *Up the River*, would have a lasting impact on his life. The film was directed by John Ford, who was to become one of the greatest directors Hollywood would ever see, and it was on this shoot that Bogie met Spencer Tracy. The two men became inseparable and together they drank Hollywood dry. Their friendship would last a lifetime.

Bogie's friendship with Spencer Tracy was one of the few positive things that he was able to take from his early foray into Hollywood. He was a fish out of water in Tinseltown and despite the attractive salary, life on the Fox lot was unfulfilling. And word from back home was equally discouraging too. Not only was Mary enthusiastically making the best of their open relationship, but Bogie's parents were feeling the pinch of the Depression. Belmont's precarious health was in terminal decline and the couple were eventually forced to sell their upscale Manhattan residence and move into more humble surroundings. Belmont continued his career as a ship's physician – on freighters these days rather than luxury liners – and at home the Bogarts lived a strange sort of life. When Belmont was in New York, he kept his own apartment in the same building as Maud, and she visited daily to cook his meals before going back to her studio to earn the money that paid his medical bills.

The Bogart family fortune was gone, leaving Maud to bear the brunt. She slept only five hours a night and was reduced to counting every cent, a practice she continued even when Bogie had made it big and moved her into a luxurious apartment in California. Maud ventured out of her studio only to tend Belmont, who was otherwise left alone to self-medicate with morphine. By the time they were sharing a single floor of a once genteel brownstone on East 56th Street, the 55 acres by the lake and that opulent New York home of Humphrey Bogart's childhood were nothing but memories.

If life in New York was uninspiring, things weren't going better in Hollywood. After a year in the California sunshine, Bogie had failed to make an impact. His last film under contract was *Bad Sister*, a flop in which he appeared alongside Bette Davis, who was making her ill-fated screen debut. Less than eighteen months after he had arrived out west hoping to make a splash, Fox declined to renew his contract; Humphrey Bogart headed home to New York.

Bogie arrived back in Manhattan at the height of the Depression, lonely and battered by his experience in California. His excursion to Los Angeles had been filled with booze and disappointment rather than laurels and leading roles and he found nothing in New York to salve his misery. Revelling in the freedom her open marriage afforded, Mary was embroiled in a passionate romance with actor Roland Young, but Bogie was determined to win her back. That he was successful suggests that Mary had at least missed her husband, and Bogie was buoyed not only by the revival of his marriage, but by the few theatrical roles he was able to land. Convinced that Hollywood wasn't for him, he swore to stick to theatre from then on.

None of the shows took off and Bogie and Mary began hitting the bottle ever harder. When Mary got a summer stock job in New England, the couple enjoyed a brief respite from the stresses of city life, but by the time they returned to New York, the lights of Broadway and the Bogarts' bank balance were both lower than ever. Bogie's game-changing Hollywood salary was gone; now he was making $50 on a good week, playing chess for money in Manhattan dives.

It was Bogie's darkest hour. In 1940, when the tough times were just bad memories, the actor penned an essay for *Screen Book* in which he reflected on 'Why Hollywood Hates Me'. In it he recalled his first disastrous foray out west and recalled that Hollywood 'crucified me when I was on the skids'.[23] But for the battle-worn actor it was a valuable lesson; even at his most successful, he never fell for the Hollywood dream again.

As Bogie tramped the streets seeking out chess games that might put a few cents in his pocket, life in the family's shared apartment was growing ever more tense. Belmont was by now an invalid, making it through the day thanks only to a morphine habit that Maud shared. Sometimes they even injected one another in front of horrified witnesses, who could hardly believe how far the once glittering couple had fallen. They were joined in their misery by Bogart's alcoholic sister, Kay, whose career as a fashion model had been brought to a shuddering halt by the Depression. For Pat, things were no better. Her marriage to Stuart Rose had seemingly been happy, but after the birth of the couple's second child, Pat slipped into depression. She was eventually committed and demanded that Stuart divorce her despite his protestations. It was a defeated Bogie and Mary who moved into the apartment with Kay, Maud and Belmont, determined not to succumb to the misery that blighted the rest of the family.

Chess and card games could only carry a man so far and when Bogie was offered a part in *After All*, a new play due to open in late 1931, he took it. It was a fateful decision. *After All* flopped, closing within a month, but in the audience one night was a scout from Columbia. He offered Humphrey Bogart a six-month contract, though he would be on loan to Warner Bros throughout, and a salary of $750 a week. This time, when Bogie packed his bags and left for Hollywood, Mary went with him. They were desperate for a brand-new start.

Instead, Bogart's bad luck chased him across the continent and he arrived in Los Angeles at the precise moment that the Depression devastated the film industry too. Across the country movie houses fell dark as audiences chose essentials over entertainment. Despite Bogie making an impression in gangster film *Three on a Match*, there was no prospect that Hollywood would capitalise on him. The salaries of major stars were being slashed and for players on six-month contracts, the future was bleak. When his contract expired, Bogie was released. He headed home to New York and the treadmill of auditions, hopeful openings and early closings. He managed to land a role in *Midnight*, a psychological thriller filmed in New York, but it was a minor picture despite an intriguing premise and a meaty role for Bogie. He needed a break desperately.

Duke Mantee

Belmont DeForest Bogart died on 8 September 1934 with Bogie at his bedside. He was only 67 but looked years older when he took his last breaths in the Hospital for the Ruptured and Crippled, an unflinching name for a place of healing. Seconds before Belmont died, Bogie was seized by a desperate need to break from the family tradition and finally show some emotion. As Bogie whispered, 'I love you, Father,' Belmont gave a gentle smile and slipped away. He left thousands of dollars' worth of debts – all of them eventually settled by his son – and a gold ring, which Bogie inherited and never took off, no matter what role he was playing. It was a transformative moment in the history of the Bogart family and one of the rare occasions on which Maud showed a glimmer of vulnerability. 'She doubled up momentarily as if she had had the wind knocked out of her,' said Bogie. 'Then straightened and said, "Well, that's done." Nothing more. Just "That's done." She did the same thing when my kid sister Kay died.'[24] Belmont didn't live to see his son's fortunes change.

In late 1934, director Arthur Hopkins was enmeshed in the casting process for *The Petrified Forest*, a new play by Robert Emmet Sherwood. The leading role had been claimed by the co-producer Leslie Howard, but the pivotal part of escaped killer Duke Mantee had yet to be cast, and no actor in town seemed to be right for the role. Hopkins was strolling along Broadway and mulling over the problem when he happened upon a failing show called *Invitation to Murder* and took a chance on a ticket. Whilst making his way to his seat, he passed a curtain from behind which he heard 'a dry, tired voice. Instantly I knew it was the voice of Duke Mantee.'[25]

That voice belonged to Humphrey Bogart, who Hopkins remembered as 'an antiquated juvenile who had spent most of his stage life in white pants and swinging a tennis racket. He seemed as far from the cold-blooded killer as one could get, but the voice persisted and the voice was Mantee's.'[26] Bogart was called in to audition and turned up looking every inch the escaped convict, sporting a three-day growth of beard and drawing on every struggle he had ever known to convince playwright Sherwood, his sometime drinking buddy, that he could play Mantee. Sherwood wondered if his friend might be better suited to a minor role and Bogie was wont to agree, admitting – ironically, given how his career would pan out – that 'I couldn't picture myself playing a gangster'.[27] But Hopkins's mind was made up – nobody else could embody Mantee, and nobody else would. It was the role that changed Humphrey Bogart's life.

> The best work of the evening is contributed by . . . Humphrey Bogart [who] has been saddled with a long line of stuffed-shirt roles, [and] is allowed to show what he can do as the killer. He can do plenty, turning in a detailed, effective and altogether grand characterization.[28]

The Petrified Forest changed everything. Years of struggle and booze had long since stripped Bogie of the juvenile good looks that had seen him bound across countless stages to ask, 'Anyone for tennis?' and left behind a man who seemed to be the physical embodiment of despair. Bogie had already played a couple of villainous roles, but his performance as Mantee was far beyond any of them. The play was the biggest hit Bogart had ever had and he knew better than to squander his success. He had paid his dues and lived his wild years and there was no repeat of the old drinking binges that had once left Mary Boland so furious. 'I can't bat around at night lapping up champagne cocktails and do good work the next day,' he told a journalist, when questioned about his work ethic. 'As far as I'm concerned, work is not just a dull interlude between parties.'[29] When Bogie made appearances in the gossip columns these days, it wasn't for his hellraising, but his beard.

> Humphrey (Hump) Bogart, who enacts killer Duke Mantee in '*The Petrified Forest*', Broadhurst, N.Y., sports a four-day growth of beard. It is a fixed part of the makeup and will be retained during the run of the play. Actor discovered he can maintain the beard at the required length by using a No. 3 barber's clipper.
> Bogart doesn't mind putting on his tux at social affairs despite the whiskers, but admits he's a bit leery wife Mary Phillips [*sic*] may mistake him for a bum.[30]

There was no mistaking Humphrey Bogart for a bum these days. The play was a sell-out night after night and though Leslie Howard was the headliner, Bogart was the man everybody wanted to see. The show ran for almost 200 performances and each night, lines ran around the block from the Broadhurst Theater. Co-producer Howard knew that the play could run and run, but he didn't want another actor to take the role that he had made his own and was instead considering an offer to take the play to London. Another major factor in the decision was the fact that Warner Bros had already bought the rights to *The Petrified Forest* and Howard was naturally guaranteed the lead. It made sense to him to bring the curtain down.

Bogie accepted the decision with his characteristic pragmatism, heartened by Howard's promise that the role of Mantee would be his when the movie was made. When the final-night curtain fell on *The Petrified Forest*, the fortunes of the Bogarts had turned around. Mary was starring alongside her old flame Roland Young in *A Touch of Brimstone* and Bogie had a booking in Maine alongside Sally Rand. As far as he was concerned, the future looked good. He was in for a nasty surprise.

21

Hollywood

Hollywood, Sept. 17.
Charles Grapewin has been signed by Warners for 'Petrified Forest'. Leslie Howard and Edward G. Robinson top the cast.[31]

For one who wasn't looking out for it, the casting notice was very easy to miss, but for Humphrey Bogart, it was a crushing loss. He had gone into summer stock in New England with no cares, fresh off a Broadway hit where audiences clamoured for the orchestra stalls seats that afforded a close-up look at his headline-making stubble. When the final curtain fell, Leslie Howard had promised him that nobody else would play the desperate Duke Mantee on screen, but that promise had never been backed up by a contract. It was a gentleman's agreement at best, and when Warners had purchased the film rights to *The Petrified Forest* for more than $100,000, the only promises they made were to Leslie Howard. When it came to Mantee, Jack Warner plumped for Edward G. Robinson, star of the hard-hitting gangster story, *Little Caesar*.

The news was crushing. Believing that Howard was a man of his word, Bogie contacted the star in Scotland and asked if it was too late to make a case to Warner on his behalf. Howard was just as stunned as his buddy and fired off a cable to Warner in which he warned the mogul, 'No Bogart, No Deal'. As the history of cinema tells, Leslie Howard came through. On the one hand, it was a testament to Howard's bankability that he had such pull with the studio, but on the other, Bogie's good fortune owed a lot to a fortuitous falling out behind the scenes at Warner Bros. Riding high since the success of *Little Caesar*, Edward G. Robinson was lobbying not only for equal billing with Howard, but a significant increase in his salary too. He had worked hard for his stardom and he wanted all the perks that came with it.

There was no surer way to annoy Jack Warner. He had expected gratitude and humility from Robinson, who had been transformed from a solid contract player into a star by his no-holds-barred performance as 'Rico' Bandello back in 1931, but instead the actor had overstepped the mark. When Warner received Howard's telegram, the boss's eyes lit up: what better way to put Edward G. Robinson firmly back in his place and save some money at the same time than to replace Robinson with Bogart? As far as the press knew, the decision to withdraw from *The Petrified Forest* was Robinson's and Robinson didn't much care: he'd had all the gangster roles he could stomach.

> Hollywood, Oct. 8.
> Humphrey Bogart, who steps into role passed up by Edward G. Robinson in '*Petrified Forest*,' arrives from New York tomorrow (Wednesday) with Leslie Howard.
> Bogart created the stage part he cops for the pic.[32]

Just like that, the part of Duke Mantee was once again in Bogie's hands. He would be back on the same $750 a week salary that he had taken on that earlier, ill-fated trip to Hollywood, but this time he only had a single film guarantee and less than a month of work. That contract was later extended to twenty-six weeks with an option to extend to seven years and a guaranteed incremental salary increase to more than $2,000, but Bogie didn't take that for granted. If the studio did exercise their option to keep him, he would be on a treadmill from which there was no easy escape. Studios worked their contract players hard and could suspend them or even cut them loose at any time: all the power rested in the hands of the moneymen. Yet if Bogie didn't sign, then he had nothing. As he autographed on the dotted line, a piece of advice given to him by actor Holbrook Blinn rang in his ears. 'He said, "Just keep working",' Bogart reminisced. 'If you're always busy, sometime somebody is going to get the idea that you must be good.'[33]

Though his role in *The Petrified Forest* was a pivotal one, it was far from the top of the bill. He was joined on the movie by Bette Davis, his co-star in the forgotten flop, *Bad Sister*, but this time the stars were aligned differently. Bogie knew that if he was ever going to make it in Hollywood, *The Petrified Forest* was his last chance. If he bungled it, his movie career would be over.

America had lost its innocence, if it had any in the first place. The Depression had wreaked havoc on the country and in cinemas, anti-heroes and outright criminals were commanding the box office. Stars such as Robinson, James Cagney and Paul Muni were making millions portraying mobsters and fact was echoing fiction with notorious names such as Bonnie and Clyde, John Dillinger and George 'Baby Face' Nelson filling column inches and commanding public fascination. Now it was Humphrey Bogart's turn. He poured every bit of disappointment he had ever faced, every struggle and every bitter rejection in his life into his seething, tense performance as the desperate Duke Mantee. The actor had chilled audiences on Broadway and now, on his last chance, he would thrill America.

Audiences had never seen anything like it. Mantee was a desperate man who followed his own code of honour, and the actor playing him was unlike any other star. Bogie wasn't conventionally handsome, nor was he glamourous, or possessed of a smooth speaking voice or an easy manner. With his haunted looks and hang-dog eyes, not to mention the clipped, rasping voice, he seemed to sum up the mood of the nation as it stumbled wearily from the Depression. Bogie's face was deeply expressive and full of character: it was the face of a man who had lived and it spoke to audiences who were battered from years of struggle. He would go on to reap the legacy of Duke Mantee in years' worth of films that never came close to the A-list success of *The Petrified Forest*.

Mayo

Hollywood contracts were notorious for the handcuffs they placed on the stars who signed them and in the wake of *The Petrified Forest*'s success, Warner put Bogie to work. He would spend what was left of the decade churning out B-movies in which he honed his craft, playing low-rent variations on Duke Mantee: an endless parade of sinister, sneering, creeping villains and heavies. 'It has been like doing one long picture with different characters walking in,'[34] he said, disappointed by the turn his apparent breakout role had taken.

When Mary Philips visited her husband in Los Angeles, she found him dejected and disillusioned. Mary encouraged Bogie to call it quits with Warner Bros and come back to New York, where she was starring in *The Postman Always Rings Twice*, but Bogie was never a quitter. Instead he made a counter-offer and asked Mary to settle in LA permanently, where she could set up a home and support his nascent movie career. There's no doubt that Bogie might have benefited from a stabilising influence at his Bohemian apartment in the Garden of Allah hotel, where the man who once said, 'I'm allergic to glamour. It's all they can do to keep shoes on me,'[35] could often be glimpsed wearing one of his three crumpled, thread-bare suits or motoring around the streets in a beat-up old rust bucket of a car, but that stabilising influence wasn't going to be Mary Philips. She already had a career and she'd worked hard for it; she had no plans to retire.

Mary's trip to Hollywood ended in a series of bitter arguments that made her decision easy: she was a leading lady and Bogie was unlikely to ever be more than a supporting actor. It didn't do to cross Mrs Bogart, who had once almost chewed off a policeman's finger when he arrested her for being drunk and disorderly, and Bogie gave up the fight. Mary went back to New York; the couple would never live together again.

It was whilst he was on this treadmill of B-movie heavies that Bogie bumped into Mayo Methot, with whom he was on nodding terms back in New York. Perhaps inevitably, the two east-coast exiles struck up a friendship. The mercurial Mayo had been a chorine during Bogie's Manhattan years and, just like him, she had headed to the lights of Los Angeles in search of success. Mayo was exuberant, glamorous and had a spark that drew Bogie in. Both of his marriages had been to women who could hold their own against him when it came to drink and drama, but Mayo was wilder than Helen or Mary could dream of. Bogie needed a distraction; in the last few years he had lost not only his father, but his friend, Bill Brady Jr, who was killed in a house fire, and his sister, Kay, who died of a ruptured appendix. Mayo was all the distraction he could wish for.

Maud and Pat moved out to Hollywood, where Bogie installed his sister and mother in their own apartments. Maud was supposedly only in Los Angeles for a holiday, but once she was settled in the Chateau Marmont, she never went home. Instead, Lady Maud became the queen of Schwab's Pharmacy, where she cut a striking figure in her white and lavender gowns as she held court amongst the Hollywood hopefuls. She even showed some uncharacteristic pride in her son, telling everyone she encountered that she was Humphrey Bogart's mother. Perhaps the west coast sun had softened her up, because Maud had never seemed proud of anything until then. Stoic to the end, Maud kept her counsel even when she fell ill in 1940 and maintained her stiff upper lip until it was too late to seek treatment. 'She died as she had lived,' said her admiring son, 'with guts.'[36]

Yet for now, Maud was the queen of Schwab's and Bogie's star was on the ascendant: he was finally able to breathe financially, if not artistically. The day-to-day struggle to keep his head above water professionally was over, so when Mayo Methot set her sights on him, he was happy to capitulate to her advances. Bogie didn't let the fact that Mayo was married stop him either, and their affair was intense, passionate and boozy. Always boozy.

Nobody was more surprised than Bogie when Mary Philips showed up in Los Angeles at the Garden of Allah, looking for a reconciliation. *The Postman Always Rings Twice* had not been the hit she was hoping for and perhaps she had heard gossip about her husband and Mayo, because she intended to stick around. Just as Bogie and Mary were playing house in their newly rented home, Mayo filed for divorce and sat tight. All she had to do was wait for the ailing Bogart marriage to tank, and tank it did as Mary ran back to the arms of Kenneth MacKenna, tired of her husband's obvious devotion to the former chorine. The divorce was finalised in 1938 and almost immediately, two August weddings were held. One was between Mary and MacKenna, the other, 'Mayo Methot to Humphrey Bogart, Aug. 20, in Los Angeles. Both in Pictures'.[37]

In Mayo, with her curious cocktail of worldliness, rage and devotion, Bogie believed that he had finally found a woman to come home to. '[Mayo] made the greatest sacrifice for him – her career ... There was nothing he needed from her, and nothing she could give, except her love,'[38] as one celebrity profile breathlessly put it. Yet there was some truth in that, because Mayo set aside her own career to create a domestic sanctuary at the couple's Horn Street home. They shared the house with a menagerie of pets and dinner was on the table promptly every night, whilst social occasions were plentiful and weekends and holidays were spent on Bogie's newly purchased boat. He relaxed by reading voraciously, always conscious that he had ducked out on his schooling and still striving to educate himself. Though the B-movies might be grinding him down, home life should have been idyllic.

'Murder and love can be interesting ... but not in front of a camera.'[39] And Bogie would soon find that out. When Mayo was sober, she was generous, smart and witty, but when Mayo drank, she drank. And when Mayo drank, she got jealous, and when she got jealous, she got violent. At the couple's home above the Sunset Strip, nightly wars raged, fuelled by Mayo's terror that Bogie would abandon her. She was suspicious of every woman her husband even so much as glanced at and if he had a love scene to shoot, Mayo treated it like the end of the world. Preoccupied by her fears of abandonment, she even resorted to paying a private eye to follow him around, but Bogie got wind of it and called the PI's agency. 'Hello, this is Humphrey Bogart,' he said. 'You got a man on my tail. Would you check with him and find out where I am?' Perhaps inevitably, Mayo's drunken insults eventually escalated into physical attacks that left her husband bruised and battered. He'd never known anything like it.

In an attempt to make light of Mayo's violent outbursts, Bogie nicknamed her Madam and, perhaps less charmingly, Sluggy, a name she shared with one of their dogs and their 30-foot cruiser. She called her husband the Bogeyman. 'Their neighbours were lulled to sleep,' said Dorothy Parker, 'by the sounds of breaking china and crashing glass.' In honour of their home's dubious status as ground zero of the war,

Bogie christened the house Sluggy Hollow, whilst the press were equal parts shocked and amused by the Battling Bogarts. But this was no joke.

The Bogarts were ugly drunks and their brawls inevitably spilled out of Sluggy Hollow into the bars and restaurants of Los Angeles. During a trip to New York, one particularly protracted confrontation erupted backstage during a personal appearance at the Strand Theatre, tumbled out into Madison Square Gardens, saw skirmishes in the 21 Club, then ended in a truce in a suite at the Algonquin Hotel. Of course, this paled in comparison to an ongoing battle that criss-crossed the United States during a star-studded publicity junket for Errol Flynn's 1939 picture, *Dodge City*. The Bogarts fought their way from LA to Kansas and home again, all smiles and loving looks on stage and all flying fists and bitter words behind the scenes. Their fights could start in the most bucolic of surroundings too, such as the afternoon's boating that ended when Mayo punched Bogie in the face with such force that he lost control of the vessel and ploughed it into the dock.

It wasn't only Mayo's husband who attracted her ire either. Occasionally drunks tried to pick a fight with Bogie, believing he was one of the hardmen he played on screen, but they always regretted it. It wasn't Bogart who waded in but Mayo, and she saw his attackers off with her fist or even the tip of her high-heeled shoe. A photograph of the Bogarts attending the premiere of *The Old Maid* in autumn 1939 shows a couple who look as though they have been married for decades… and not happily. Swathed in fur, Mayo wears a half smile and stares fixedly out of the frame, whilst Bogie makes insolent eye contact with the camera lens. His face is granite hard, every inch the tough guy his audiences believed him to be. Mayo, of course, knew different.

It was always Bogie who got the worst of their fights. Mayo would go wild with anger, waving guns, threatening to cut her wrists or even setting fire to the house during one drunken rage, yet Bogart tried to be pragmatic. He claimed that their fights invigorated him, but it must have been utterly exhausting. 'We fight to stay married,'[40] he told his friends with a gallows humour that could only take him so far. Bogie swore he found Mayo's jealous rages sexy and Hollywood lore is filled with stories of her hurling bottles or even plates full of Thanksgiving dinner in front of guests. The fights became such a sideshow that Bogie would merely replate the food and sit down to dine as though nothing had happened. In restaurants they slung crockery and glassware and, on one occasion, Bogie was chatting on the telephone to a friend when there was a crash in the background. Without missing a beat, he informed his buddy that Mayo had hurled an ashtray at his head. When it sailed harmlessly past, Bogie could only worry why her aim had gotten so poor.

And then there were the weapons. Luckily, Mayo's aim was off when she pulled a gun on Bogie, but she was right on target with the knife she thrust into her husband's back. Miraculously, the resulting injury was only a flesh wound. Both Mayo and Bogie tried to pass their clashes off as quirky fun, but when Mayo told a journalist that 'Boogie [*sic*] has thrown away some of the best scenes of his career arguing with me in the living room,'[41] her black humour masked a destructive truth. Far from supporting her husband, she dismissed him as a 'cheap, ham actor', attacking one of the few things Bogie truly felt he excelled at. Something had to give.

Whenever Bogie's business took him to New York, rumour had it that he headed straight to the home of his first wife, Helen Menken, who was by now happily remarried. Bogart wasn't looking for a hook-up, but Helen's easy company provided a welcome respite from Mayo's drama. Yet Bogie and Mayo's reconciliations rivalled their fights in passion and she revelled in being married to a husband who behaved as she believed a real man should: that drunken rages and week-long fights weren't everyone's idea of a masculine ideal never so much as occurred to her.

Whilst all of this was going on, Humphrey Bogart was enjoying a taste of real movie stardom, albeit with crumbs from the table of bigger stars like Robinson or Cagney. 'In the first 34 pictures,' he said, 'I was shot in 12, electrocuted or hanged in 8, and was a jailbird in 9.'[42] He was given a rare leading role whilst on loan to Metro-Goldwyn-Mayer for *Dead End* in 1937, but thanks to his straitjacket of a contract, two-thirds of his salary went to Warners. As Bogie's star rose, he and Warner Bros were in constant dispute over money and script quality: the star wanted more cash and better films, but the studio weren't about to cave in, not when they had him on the hook for seven years. Bogart even acknowledged that 'I'm known as the guy who always squawks about roles, but never refuses to play one.'[43] Through it all, Bogie recalled Blinn's words: 'Just keep working.'

High Sierra

Humphrey Bogart was the first choice when it came to second-string gangsters; he provided reliable support for big-name actors who snagged the leads he was so hungry for. Bogie performed in a musical, a Western, even a horror film that saw him sport badger-striped hair, and with each role it seemed ever more likely that he would never get that elusive A-list break. *High Sierra* was the film that changed all that. John Huston's well-thumbed script already bore the fingerprints of Jimmy Cagney, Edward G. Robinson and George Raft, all of whom had turned it down, but when Bogie heard that the part was going begging, he knew he had to have it. It was a turning point in his career.

If *The Petrified Forest* had been a blazing introduction, then *High Sierra* was the film that proved once and for all that Humphrey Bogart was more than a second-string gangster. In the role of bank robber Roy Earle – ably supported by the leading man's own dog, Zero, as Pard – Bogie once again turned in a performance that was as sensitive and layered as it was glowering and vital. In Huston's script, adapted from W.R. Burnett's eponymous novel, Earle was no one dimensional crook, but a man with an intriguing past, and Bogart brought that complex character blazing into life.

Tainted by his career in B-movies, Bogie lost out on top billing to Ida Lupino, but adoring reviews left no doubt as to who was the true star of the movie. He was well-served by director Raoul Walsh's treatment of Huston's screenplay, which combined with Bogie's performance to elevate the film into a masterpiece of tension. Yet Bogie's second billing wasn't just down to star power: a political wrangle had marked him as damaged goods. The actor was identified as someone who had attended secret meetings of Hollywood subversives – Communists – and he was asked to name names. Bogie refused and fought the accusations with typical pugnacity, channelling his fury into work, but the experience left him ruffled and angry and years later, he and Lauren Bacall would speak out against the Hollywood witch hunts. It was enough to ensure that there would be no top billing on *High Sierra*; in future films, he would receive nothing *but* top billing.

Released in 1941, *High Sierra* was the swansong of the American gangster picture. It arrived in cinemas as the war in Europe was raging and American involvement was a hot topic of conversation. Suddenly the likes of Al Capone didn't seem like the towering villains they once been, not when held up against Adolf Hitler. Critics couldn't praise Bogie highly enough, but if the gangster movie was dead, then what next for Humphrey Bogart? As the ticket dollars rolled in and the adoring reviews piled up, the perennial second-stringer was a star in a genre that was facing its final curtain. Bogie just had to hold on and ride the wave as studios clamoured to borrow him from Warners and he found himself inundated with offers that saw his agent, Sam Jaffe, juggling everything from movies to personal appearances to cigarette ads. These were especially lucrative, because performers were allowed to keep the majority of the revenue from such endeavours so long as they donated a portion to charities of Jack Warner's choosing.

Bogie expected to find the world at his feet, but instead the hapless contract player found himself cast in *The Wagons Roll at Night*, an uninspiring tale of murder at a travelling carnival. For the first time, the man who always kept working refused to do so. Depressed by the projects on offer and the death of his mother in 1940, Bogie took off on his boat. The studio answered by placing him on suspension; it was a stalemate.

The Studios

Long before movie studios were pawns and money-makers in the hands of enormous multinationals, the Hollywood studio system reigned supreme. In the golden era of Hollywood, the major players in town were the Big Five – MGM, Paramount, Warner Bros, 20th Century Fox and RKO. Below them were Universal, Columbia, and United Artists, and from there the quality declined until it reached Poverty Row, where the likes of Monogram churned out cheapies.

Until a 1948 Supreme Court ruling forced studios to separate production from distribution and exhibition, the Big Five effectively controlled American cinema through a stranglehold system of vertical integration, which allowed them to make movies on their own lots using creatives who were signed to long-term contracts and paid a salary, rather than a fee per film. These contracts invariably placed all the power in the hands of the studio and were the source of much dissatisfaction for actors, who were not allowed to choose their own projects. Nor could they take work from outside studios without complicated agreements that were usually lucrative for their home studio, but rarely for the actors themselves. The studios then released the films they had made to their own cinemas, whilst offering them to independent cinemas via a system of block booking, forcing picture houses to take not only the big hits, but the also-ran support features too. Namely, the A and B-movies.

Like so many others who had been signed to studio contracts, the initial thrill of a guaranteed salary and regular work soon gave way to the harsh reality of the Hollywood star and studio system for Bogie. Unable to choose his own projects and held in contractual handcuffs, he had two choices. He could shut up and take the roles he was offered, none of which showcased the remarkable skills he had demonstrated in *The Petrified Forest* and *High Sierra*, or he could be placed on suspension and not work at all. By now Bogart's salary was in excess of $60,000 per movie and he knew that suspension was a risky business. It effectively left an actor in limbo and the knock-on effect was that they were soon forgotten by the public and advertisers alike, so those lucrative extra-curricular gigs quickly dried up too. It was alien to Bogie, who had always kept on grafting.

Not so long ago, Bogie had admitted that 'I don't believe in taking suspensions. When you go on suspension for refusing a role, you go out of circulation. And what happens when you go back? You get the same part in another picture.'[44] Only a year had passed since he uttered those words, but Bogie's attitude had changed. Safe in the knowledge that he had some clout, he accepted the suspension. As he sailed out into the ocean, he was determined to wait out his punishment for as long as it took.

The Maltese Falcon

As Bogie contemplated the empty horizon, in Hollywood the machine kept on churning until *The Maltese Falcon* made its way to the front of the line. John Huston, Bogart's collaborator and drinking buddy, had written a screenplay from Dashiell Hammett's novel and was signed up to direct. Warner had already lined up George Raft for the plum role of Sam Spade, but Raft exercised a no-remake clause in his contract and turned the movie down, unwilling to work with the inexperienced Huston. Since *The Maltese Falcon* had been filmed before on more than one occasion, the star cut the script loose.

Warner Bros might never have considered Bogie for *The Maltese Falcon* at all were it not for the fact that the actor, by now in his 40s, far from movie-star handsome and seemingly unable to get a break, had tapped into an audience that all studios wanted to capitalise on: women. Bogie's personal appearances were swamped by adoring female fans and where adoring female fans went, ticket sales followed. The suspension had been intended to teach the recalcitrant actor a lesson and *The Maltese Falcon* was the olive branch that was expected to lure him in, suitably chastened. But Bogie didn't come back because he feared suspension: what drew him back was the chance to work with Huston again. Humphrey Bogart would become not only the quintessential Sam Spade, but the quintessential noir detective, setting a benchmark that has rarely been equalled.

As the third movie adaptation of Hamnett's work, *The Maltese Falcon* could have faced an ignominious fate. Initially filmed in 1931 as a Bebe

Daniels/Ricardo Cortez-starring vehicle, then again as a knockabout comedy named *Satan Met a Lady* in 1936, the book had so far not fared well on screen. To chance a third version in a decade was quite a gamble, and it was compounded by the decision to cast an actor better known for villains than heroes in the central role as Sam Spade. Luckily, Huston caught lightning in a bottle. The shoot took less than a month and was a tour de force of moviemaking and performance; everything came together to make a classic.

> This is one of the best examples of actionful and suspenseful melo-dramatic story telling in cinematic form. Unfolding a most intriguing and entertaining murder mystery, picture displays outstanding excellence in writing, direction, action and editing – combining overall as a prize package of entertainment for wildest audience appeal. Due for hefty grosses in all runs, it's textured with ingredients presaging numerous holdover in the keys and strong word-or-mouth will make the b.o. wickets spin ... Of major importance is the stand-out performance of Humphrey Bogart, an attention arresting portrayal that will add immeasurable voltage to his marquee values. Bogart not only dominates the proceedings throughout, but is the major motivation in all but a few minor scenes.[45]

Despite his professional triumph, Bogart's transformation into a gruff but sensitive hero didn't go down well at home. Bogie had never been comfortable with love scenes, self-deprecatingly claiming that 'I couldn't see myself holding some dizzy dame in my arms, murmuring a lot of corny bilge into her ear,'[46] but *The Maltese Falcon* proved the lie to his claims that 'they won't make a Great Lover out of me if I can help it'.[47] Mayo was proud of her husband's achievements, but his love scenes with Mary Astor drove Mrs Bogart into a jealous, violent frenzy even as they electrified the screen.

No longer a second-string gangster, Bogie would stay on the A-list for the rest of his life. In movies such as *All Through the Night* he was still picking up George Raft's rejects, yet they offered a change from the usual heavies. Now his heroes might be troubled, drunk or as anti as they come, but they were still heroes. But even as work was flourishing, at home things were getting worse by the day; on more than one occasion, Bogie turned up on set exhausted from being forced to sleep outside or battered physically and emotionally from yet another argument. By the time he starred in his iconic role as Rick Blaine in *Casablanca*, the marriage was on the out.

A hysterical Mayo told people that her husband had fallen out of love with her and honestly, after years of mutual combat, it was hardly surprising.

There is a curious addendum to Bogart's love life that bears a mention here. In the 1980s, Verita Thompson, Bogie's personal hairdresser on more than a dozen movies, published an autobiographical tell-all about an alleged long-term love affair with the actor. Bogie was pouring his heart out to Helen Menken and plenty of other women during the collapse of his marriage, but whether Verita Thompson was one of them is open to conjecture. In her memoir, Thompson claimed that Bacall okayed the affair in return for unbridled access to her husband's bankroll, but whilst an on-set liaison with a hairdresser isn't unheard of, one that lasted for fourteen years is a little more doubtful. Bogie's years with Bacall were his most contented, but during his marriage to Mayo, his personal life was in freefall.

Casablanca

Bogart had been on the outside looking in for too long. As one magazine asked in 1943, 'Isn't it time, now that Bogart has definitely proved his value, to give him something to do that may make film history?'[48] Time would tell that he had already achieved that with *The Maltese Falcon*; the decades that followed would make him a legend, and *Casablanca* was one of the foundations of that myth. It came at precisely the right moment for American audiences too, who flocked to the movie aflame with patriotic fervour, eager to see Bogie give the Nazis a bloody nose.

Helmed by Michael Curtiz, *Casablanca* gave Bogie the opportunity to work with his good friend Peter Lorre, but more importantly, it gave him a chance to build a role from the ground up. He would earn nearly $37,000 for playing the world-weary Rick Blaine, and receive one of his favourite pieces of fan mail into the bargain. 'I saw your picture "Casablanca" in Oran, and now that I'm in Casablanca, I want to say that the town looks just like it did in the movie,' wrote a GI stationed in North Africa. 'But what I'd like to know is, where the h[ell] is Ingrid Bergman?'

Though the movie bought its lighter moments, it caused Bogie headaches at home. Mayo took one look at Ingrid Bergman, who played the torn-between-two-men role of Ilsa Lund, and immediately identified her as a threat. During shooting, Bergman saw little of Bogie, who spent so long in his trailer that she concluded that he must dislike her. In fact, it was easier for Bogie to hide away from Bergman than to befriend her and pour more fuel on the fire of Mayo's jealousy. *Casablanca* gave the world one of the most iconic movie couples in Hollywood history, but all Mayo saw was danger. She couldn't recognise the line between fact and fiction, and her husband's transformation from heavy to heartthrob only inflamed her jealousy further. Mayo never saw his sex-symbol status coming; nobody did, least of all Bogart. By now in his 40s, lisping, scarred and wearing every disappointment on his face, he was no handsome Errol Flynn type. But Flynn fans were already well catered for and in an America that was hungry for heroes, Humphrey Bogart was everything that the moviegoing public wanted. The film was a hit. *Casablanca* earned Bogie his first Oscar nomination and a new contract valued at $195,000 per year.

Bogie followed *Casablanca* with *Action in the North Atlantic*, a workaday piece of patriotism that pitted the Allies against the Nazis and as soon as that had wrapped, he was off to Columbia on loan for another bit of cinematic patriotism called *Sahara*. This time there were no women in the cast, but Mayo still found plenty to carp about.

By now, Mayo was drinking every evening and the couple were fighting constantly, both physically and verbally. The last role Bogie wanted was one in which he was constantly battling a movie wife too; of course, that's precisely what he was offered.

On Tour

For Bogart, acting had been an escape from marital strife, so when he was offered *Conflict*, in which an unhappy husband murders his nagging wife so he can woo her charming sister, he turned it down. He was keen to start shooting as soon as possible on *Passage to Marseille*, which would reunite director Curtiz and star Bogart with the mainstays of the *Casablanca* cast, including Peter Lorre, Claude Rains, and Sydney Greenstreet, and *Conflict* was an unwanted distraction. Perhaps Bogie believed that his star status, not to mention an Oscar nomination and a legion of fans, might mean that he was no longer beholden to Jack Warner. If so, he was wrong. 'Humphrey Bogart once said I was a creep,' teased an amused Warner, but the mogul cared more about money than making friends with his star. Warner would reunite Bogie and Sydney Greenstreet all right, but not in the wartime intrigue of *Passage to Marseille*, at least not until Greenstreet had played the man who uncovers Bogart's murderous crimes in *Conflict*.

Warner had suspended Bogart before and would do it again if he refused *Conflict*. If he was placed on suspension, *Passage to Marseille* hung in the balance too: either it wouldn't go into production at all, or it would do so without Bogie. At first Bogie stuck to his guns, telling Warner, 'I just can't do it ... I am an honest man and I have to be honest with myself.' But he had underestimated Jack Warner's need to be obeyed; no *Conflict*, said the boss, no *Passage to Marseille*. With a heavy heart, Bogie signed on to the middling noir. His performance was one of the few standout elements of the film, which sat on the shelf for two years until Warner Bros finally wound down its output of war films and used the slush pile to plug the gaps.

Though Bogie had looked forward to shooting *Passage to Marseille*, when filming began he was at his lowest ebb. He always turned up on time and with his lines learned, but he often stank of booze and looked as though he'd slept under a hedge. Just as Bergman had found him withdrawn during the shooting of *Casablanca*, now he was despondent and introverted, coming out of himself only when knocking back liquor with his friend Lorre. Knocking back liquor was also a key part of Bogie and Mayo's 1944 USO tour of North Africa and Italy, where they played the happy couple for audiences before resuming hostilities behind closed doors. After a wild night in Naples, the couple held a party for soldiers in their room that got out of hand. The festivities culminated in the Bogarts firing live ammunition into the ceiling, enraging the military brass who were sharing the hotel.

In his memoir, partygoer John Huston recalled that Bogie was asked to apologise to the senior officers whose sleep had been disturbed. 'Bogie answered appropriately with something like "Go fuck yourself".'[49] Within days, the Bogarts were on their way home to the US.

The press, meanwhile, played the whole thing for laughs... but after his wife had literally stabbed him in the back, no doubt Bogie was relieved that it was only the fixtures and fittings that Mayo had peppered with lead.

> Untrue, no doubt, but hilarious is the story going the rounds about the overseas entertainment tour of the Battling Bogarts. By their own admission, Humphrey and Mayo battle more than any other happily married couple in Hollywood. During their tour of Italy they lived for several days in a bomb damaged hotel in Naples. The place was practically falling apart but the army had taken it over as the best available under the circumstances. After six days in the war-torn hotel, according to the story, the Bogarts were handed a bill by the army for damage done to their room![50]

When the Bogarts landed in America, Bogie disappeared into New York to join Helen Menken. He knew that he would soon be back on a film set, but he was keen to put some distance between himself and Mayo before he returned to the Hollywood machine for another noir, this one co-starring a complete unknown.

Hollywood, Sept. 26.

Warners increased its list of prospective femme stars to 17 with the signing of Dorothy Malone to a long-term pact.

Other youngsters under grooming on the Burbank lot are Colleen Townsend, Lauren Bacall, Tessa Brind, Virginia Patton, Janis Paige, Andrea King, Angela Green, Faye Emerson, Pat Clark, Lynne Bagget [*sic*], Joan McCracken, Dolores Moran, Jean Sullivan, Joan Winfield and Berry Alexander.[51]

Variety's list of new starlets under contract to Warner Bros in 1944 contains a wealth of stories in itself. Some of the newcomers went on to tragedy and some to success, including Dorothy Malone, who could match Bogie for early-career struggles. Malone battled against B-movie oblivion to win an Oscar for the Douglas Sirk classic *Written on the Wind* in 1957, eclipsing her co-star, Lauren Bacall. Yet it was Bacall who would become Bogie's Mrs Me, as famous for The Look and her love life as her career. Lauren Bacall was to make her debut opposite Humphrey Bogart in his next picture, *To Have and Have Not*. It would change both their lives forever.

Act Two

Bacall

'When I think back on it now I wonder if it really all happened to me or if it wasn't someone else.'[1]

Betty Joan

Humphrey Bogart struggled for four decades to find his place in the world. He was the newcomer who was anything but, his success coming after years of plugging away, struggling and knocking at the door, hoping that someone in Hollywood would haul him clear of the B-movies and second-string gangsters that seemed to be his destiny. For Lauren Bacall, things were different. Success found her early, but proved harder to sustain. For years, she pushed against the title of Mrs Bogart, though it was the title she loved most of all.

The vampish Lauren Bacall was hewn from Betty Joan Perske, who was born in the Bronx, New York City, on 16 September 1924. Unlike Bogart, whose family could – and did – romance their lineage back through the generations, Betty had no such claims to be one of the settling families of New York. Her mother, Natalie Weinstein-Bacal, left Romania as a baby, carried by a family that had lost everything. The Bacal name was eliminated from official paperwork by an overworked Ellis Island administrator and the Weinsteins settled in a New York tenement. Betty's grandfather, Max, pushed a sales cart loaded with household essentials from street to street all day long until he could exchange the tenement for a humble apartment and the cart for a confectionary shop. Plagued by ill health and working long hours to improve the lot of the Weinstein family, when Max was just 55 he took a nap after a rare visit to the movies; he never woke up.

As a widow with five young children, Max's wife Sophie faced an uncertain future when she took over the family business, but under her ownership, it flourished. Stepping out from another upgraded apartment, Betty's mother Natalie was employed as a secretary when she met salesman William Perske. The couple were married and started a family, but their romance soon soured. Perske had a violent temper and subjected Natalie to brutal beatings, leaving her terrified that her baby might suffer the same fate. When Perske threatened Betty with a whipping, Natalie swung into action. She packed the 6-year-old off to rural New York, where she would be safe in the care of her extended family. While Betty was gone, Natalie filed for divorce.

William was already a shadowy figure in Betty's life and now he became almost totally absent. For a couple of years, he visited his daughter each Sunday but eventually even those grudging visits dried up. In her autobiography, Bacall remembered a cheap watch that her father gave her on one of those Sundays. Though it wasn't valuable, she was so worried about damaging or losing the all-too-rare token of affection that she asked her mother to look after it. When William found out, he snatched the gift back: though Natalie never tried to turn Betty against her father, he was happy to play the villain all on his own.

Perhaps inevitably, when Betty Perske, by then sultry, sexy Lauren Bacall, married Humphrey Bogart, there were those who speculated that their romance was the culmination of her search for a father figure. She was 19, after all, whilst he was 45, but this is to ignore the influence that Natalie had on her daughter. Betty's father was absent, but Natalie more than made up for it when she took back the name her family had lost at Ellis Island and became Natalie Bacal, an identity all of her own. Little Betty Bacal was an honorary member of her mother's inner circle, a gathering of close female friends who neither had nor wanted a man in their lives. Just like Betty in the years to come, Natalie would never settle for second best; if she ever gave her heart again, it had to be to a man worthy not only of her, but of her daughter too.

Bogie's childhood had created a distance between the little boy and his parents, but Natalie and Betty's relationship was as close as could be. Though Natalie couldn't afford a Bogart-sized roster of starch-aproned nurses and domestics, she lavished Betty with love and affection instead. Natalie taught her that hard work, humour and honour were the most important weapons anyone could have in their arsenal, and she made sure her daughter knew there were consequences if she stepped out of line. When Betty stole a pencil case from a five and dime, Natalie marched her protesting daughter right back to the store and had her apologise; it was a lesson well learned. Most importantly, she wanted Betty to know that the world was hers to conquer: she could be anything she wanted to be, and that included a star.

Many people have ascribed Bacall's infamous pragmatism to Bogie's influence but perhaps it started earlier than that. Natalie encouraged and supported her daughter's dreams, but she never pretended that success would come easy. It was important to Natalie that her daughter recognise not only her self-worth, but that there were limits. 'You had it drummed into your head from childhood by your mother, grandmother, uncles,' Bacall said, 'that nice Jewish girls didn't smoke – weren't fast – nice Jewish girls had character.'[2] But nice Jewish girls could also have ambition, so long as they had humility to go with it. Betty Bacal was no Baby Jane, despite her mother's decision to enrol her in dance classes, alongside her friends from the neighbourhood.

As a single parent in the city, Natalie had no choice but to work if she wanted to keep up her household. At first, she employed a maid to meet Betty each afternoon after school, but after the maid locked her little charge in a closet, another solution had to be found. Just like Bogie, Betty was a prime candidate for boarding school, but unlike him there was no fortune to fall back on. Instead, generous loans from family were offered and Natalie scraped together enough to send her 8-year-old daughter to Highland Manor, a school for girls in Tarrytown, New York.

If Bogie's schooldays had been a laundry list of failures and dropouts, Betty's were anything but. Though her ambitions were to be a singer or actress, she had a keen academic mind and proved to be such a scholar that she was able to graduate a year earlier than the rest of her class. She certainly excelled when compared to the held-back Bogie.

Wearing his fedora and permanent scowl, Bogie found it difficult to make friends among the boys in his grade. This wasn't a problem that afflicted Betty. Outgoing, sporty and popular, she had no trouble finding confidantes amongst her peers. In fact, the only thing she really shared with Bogie during those school years was the fact that both loved drama. He in the little performances his gang put on with costumes borrowed from Bill Brady Sr, she in school plays and recitals. The spark of performance had already been ignited in Betty when she arrived at Highland Manor, but by the time she graduated and came home to the city, it was a fire. Betty Bacal wanted to be a ballerina, so Natalie enrolled her in classes with Mikhail Mordkin, a former partner of Anna Pavlova. It seemed as though Natalie had been telling her daughter the truth: Betty really could be anything she dreamed of.

Back home in New York, Betty and Natalie joined her grandmother and Natalie's brother, Charlie, in a shared apartment. Though it wasn't luxurious, it had one particular element that appealed to Betty: a room of her own. Bogie had his own little boat and sprawling houses in which to roam, but the tiny room in that apartment on 84th Street and West End Avenue became Betty's sanctuary. It was the first but not the last apartment that the Bacals would inhabit in New York, as Charlie's marriage and relocation forced Natalie and Betty to give up the comfortable shared apartment for something a lot cheaper.

Betty's return to the city proved to be a wakeup call. At boarding school, she had been surrounded by friends and had nothing to worry about beyond her next sporting tournament. On the streets of Manhattan, though, life for a young girl was perilous. Betty's trips to and from school were fraught with fear as men subjected her to daily harassment. Decades later, she wryly dismissed it as 'the usual', but Betty was terrified, and each time she came home trembling, Natalie moved them on until they had found a safe place on 86th Street at last. It wasn't grand by any means, but it was home, and every spare cent Natalie could save went towards prettying up their humble apartment. Meanwhile, every spare cent Betty coppered together went straight into the ticket booth of her nearest movie house. Movies were a cheap way to get a day out, and for a quarter Betty could lose herself in a hundred different worlds.

Betty and Bette

As the years passed, Betty kept on growing... and growing. She was tall, slim and totally lacking in the physical strength needed for ballet. Her fate was sealed when Mordkin told Natalie that she was wasting her money: Betty's feet were the wrong type for a ballet dancer. So Betty just adjusted her dreams. The girl who loved to while away dreary weekend afternoons in the movie house and Saturday mornings studying at the New York School of the Theatre simply replaced her ballet partner with Fred Astaire, and dreamed of tap shoes and marabou feathers instead.

Betty's ambitions were fanciful, for sure, but still she stood in marked contrast to Bogie, who didn't know what he wanted to do even when he started doing it. He didn't fall in love with performing, but fell into it, and it just so happened that it was the place he belonged. Betty, on the other hand, already knew that her future would be bright, ballet or not. The little girl who grew up watching Bette Davis on the big screen had been taught that she could do anything at all, and she was about to test that theory.

Alongside her lovingly nurtured dreams of stardom, Betty couldn't help but compare herself to leading ladies like Loretta Young and Margaret Sullivan and find herself wanting. They weren't tall and skinny like Betty, who famously said she didn't know she was coltish until a journalist told her so: she just didn't fit the mould. But Betty had always been told by Natalie that she was beautiful and we shouldn't underestimate the power of that. In a world that still tells young women how they ought to look, Betty had been given a dose of self-confidence that some people would kill for.

Perhaps one of the best demonstrations of that confidence came when Bette Davis was staying at New York's Gotham Hotel with a mutual friend of Betty Bacal's uncle Jack, himself a lawyer with entertainment connections. He engineered a brief meeting with Davis for Betty and her best friend, Betty Kalb, and the two teenagers enjoyed a private audience with their goddess. The two Betties were so starstruck that they could barely speak as their idol advised them on how much hard work and dedication it would take to make it as an actress, and they absorbed it like oxygen. Years later, Bacall and Davis met again when the latter came backstage to congratulate her now famous fan on her performance in *Applause*, a Broadway musical take on Davis's own *All About Eve*.

By the time Betty graduated, she had settled on her future career: she would become a celebrated actress, and a celebrated actress needed training. Her generous uncles came through once again and agreed to help Natalie make up the tuition fee for a place at the American Academy of Dramatic Arts, but that financial commitment would make things at home tighter than ever. If Betty got her place at the academy, her allowance would have to be slashed, and there would be no luxuries at all. But so long as she had enough for a movie ticket, Betty was happy.

Betty's entire life became the American Academy of Dramatic Arts. Bogie had never undertaken any formal training; thrust out onto the stage as an understudy, some might have soared, but he had been hobbled by stage fright. Betty, however, was being trained in every aspect of performance, from movement to monologues and beyond. It was at the academy that she started to learn other things too, and she fell hard for a senior named Kirk Douglas, who she had first seen in a play at the academy. Though Betty longed to make him her first boyfriend, their dates never progressed beyond platonic. Besides, Betty's first real passion was acting, and she loved the academy above everything. As she neared the end of her first year, however, her mother broke bad news. The family finances were stretched to the limit and there simply wasn't the money for a second year of tuition. Even worse, scholarships were only available to male students, a stinging injustice that denied Betty the second year her grades had promised. There was no other option than to get a job and leave her studies behind.

At first Betty decided to swerve into showbiz via modelling, but her efforts to join the more prestigious agencies fell flat. The models she met at her auditions advised her that more humble agencies might be willing to take a chance on her and eventually Betty found herself on Seventh Avenue at the offices of David Crystal. She walked for a panel, fibbed through an interview in which she claimed to be an actress and photographic model, and was promptly signed up on a salary of $30 a week. She was still only 16 years old.

The Garment Center

If this was a work of fiction, Betty would immediately begin booking once-in-a-lifetime jobs and sashay along the road to stardom in fine Cinderella style. Real life, however, doesn't always work that way. Surrounded by seasoned models, Betty felt more ungainly than ever and the work didn't last. She was let go on account of being too thin and underdeveloped – a polite way of saying flat-chested – to show off the fashions of the day to their best advantage. It was a hammer blow to Betty not because she loved modelling – she didn't – but because her wages had allowed her not only to contribute to the household, but to feel as though she was growing up at last. Still, she had been raised by a worker to be a worker, and before long she was modelling for another agency, whilst tirelessly pursuing acting work at the same time.

Empowered by the self-belief Natalie had instilled in her, Betty set about knocking on the door of what seemed like every producer in New York, badgering for any role she thought might be a good fit... and a few that she was pretty sure wouldn't. She further insinuated herself into the world of theatre by spending her lunchbreak selling copies of audition listing magazine *Actor's Cue* at the doorway to Sardi's, the legendary Broadway restaurant. From her pitch, she introduced herself to every producer and star who passed, hoping against hope that someone would give her a break. Nobody did.

As Bogie was struggling to make his name and America was gearing up to enter the war, Betty Bacal knew that the time had come to make a change. Tired of being pawed by buyers at the Seventh Avenue Garment Center, she gave up her modelling job to work as an usher at Broadway's

Morocco Theatre. Though the pay was a paltry $8 a week, it put Betty at the heart of theatreland, tearing tickets for *Blithe Spirit*. In a wonderful twist of fate, not so many years later Lauren Bacall would star alongside the playwright, Noël Coward, in a television production of that same play.

Given the number of self-described models currently clamouring for attention on social media, it may seem odd that Betty gave up a modelling gig to collect ticket stubs, but this wasn't modelling as we may think of it. There were no photographers, no catwalks and certainly no glamour. Modelling to buyers at the Garment Center was hard, uncomfortable work, and it could be deeply unpleasant too. The buyers always worked a season or so ahead, meaning that the models would be showcasing thin summer clothes in the freezing New York winter, and buried under winter layers in the seething summer heat. Part of the buyers' job was to feel the clothes and cloth, to check the textiles and the quality of the finish, and they frequently went far further than they should have. It's a horrible truth that the models were often subject to unwanted physical attention and the perpetrators were rarely if ever brought to book. As an usher, Betty would no longer be paraded and pawed, but instead would be in the place she loved most of all: the theatre.

Once Betty had sat in awestruck silence during her meeting with Bette Davis, but during her stint as an usher she had access to performers that the door shift at Sardi's couldn't provide. It was during those days that she befriended actor Paul Lukas, who would become a father figure to the young woman in many ways. Whenever she needed advice, it was the experienced Lukas to whom she turned. He knew the grind it took to build a career and he was happy to share the benefit of his years in the business with the starry-eyed usher.

Broadway

Yet for all of Betty's chutzpah, there were no big breaks. She eventually got a performing job of sorts as a hostess at the newly opened Stage Door Canteen in New York, but it was a long way from the stage. Betty's job was to take care of the visiting servicemen, many of whom were far from home and missing their girlfriends. The canteen offered a salubrious opportunity to dance and chat with the hostesses, but its big draw was the major movie stars who took shifts as both a thank you and a morale booster to the boys. When the stars weren't washing dishes or waiting tables, they might give an impromptu performance, and the Stage Door Canteen became a sanctuary for many young men who had never been away from home before. For Betty, it was a place to rub shoulders – however briefly – with the biggest names in showbiz.

Whilst Betty was working Monday nights at the Stage Door Canteen and ushering for $8 a week, she kept on working her shoe leather, chasing auditions all over town. Though her face was becoming known in offices up and down Broadway, the answer was always the same: we'll call you if anything comes up. It was the same answer she got from the Brown brothers, who were producing a show named *Johnny 2 × 4*, and Betty didn't expect to hear another word about it. She had long since learned not to get her hopes too high, so when she received a call back to the Brown office on 44th Street, it was like a fairy tale. The job on offer was a walk-on at $15 a week; there were no lines and no spotlight, but for the first time, Betty Bacal would be on a Broadway stage.

Now Betty set herself a goal. She gave herself a decade to make it, and she would reach her target with years to spare. With a new page in life came a new name. Betty was beginning to find Bacal a hindrance, with some people pronouncing her name Bacall and others Backle, so she added one more L to make it easier, becoming Miss Bacall at last.

Set in a speakeasy and filled with music, melodrama and comedy, *Johnny 2 × 4* cast Betty as one of ten walk-on performers who were to dance and strut, rhubarb and pose. She felt like the star of the show. Bogie once joked that he was the worst oracle of success: if he thought a project was a knockout, it bombed; if he predicted a bomb, it was a hit. Betty soon gave him a run for his money. She loved *Johnny 2 × 4* and expected a runaway success, but the critics weren't kind. The show would close after just eight weeks, then spend another month or so dragging itself around the Broadway boroughs. Betty was disappointed, but now she'd had a taste of what it meant to be a real actress, she was ready to progress from walk-ons to speaking roles.

Once again, Betty got on the treadmill of auditions, but this time she was angling to read for featured roles. When *Claudia*, a Broadway hit with Dorothy Maguire in the lead role, posted auditions for its touring production, Betty went for it. She received first one callback, then another, then a third, until her hopes were higher than they had ever been. When the moment of truth came, she was offered the chance to understudy the title role; it would take 17-year-old Betty away from home for a year and it was the biggest break she had ever been offered. The only break she had been offered. But it meant she would be off the Broadway circuit for twelve months with no guarantee that she would ever set foot on a stage. On the other hand, it was a starring role ... Feeling utterly lost, Betty called on the voice of reason. She went to see Paul Lukas.

Lukas had been around for years. He knew how fast an actor could be forgotten if he wasn't visible and he knew that the cost of not performing could be huge. After listening to Betty's dilemma, Lukas told her that only she could make the decision, but he reminded her of the time and shoe leather she'd sacrificed to get her face in front of casting directors and producers. If she disappeared to spend a year as an understudy, a host of new faces would replace hers in the memories of the Broadway titans whom she greeted outside Sardi's each lunchtime. Betty's heart was heavy, but she knew what she had to do. She turned down *Claudia*.

With her big chance gone, Betty supplemented her role in *Johnny 2 × 4* with modelling work. But whenever anyone turned a camera on her, Betty had a problem: she shook. That nervous tremble would one day prove to be the making of her. Betty was signed to Walter Thornton's agency and when she was crowned Miss Greenwich Village 1942, no doubt the fact that Walter Thornton was the judge was nothing but a very fortunate coincidence. It was hardly Miss America, but it was a small something. In fact, Betty's first review – published in *Esquire* – wasn't for a performance or a modelling job, it was as an usher: 'The Prettiest Theatre Usher: The tall, slender blonde in the St. James Theatre, right aisle, during the Gilbert & Sullivan engagement — by general rapt agreement among the critics, but the bums are too dignified to admit it.'[3]

Bogie toiled for years for to climb from the B-list to the top, but Betty didn't want to wait. She longed not just to act, but to live the lifestyle of the stars she'd met at the Stage Door Canteen, and she was offered a brief glimpse of what the future might hold in 1942, when she bumped into George Jean Nathan during a stint as a hostess at a USO benefit. Nathan was the critic who had given her ushering such a glowing write-up, and he introduced her to Burgess Meredith. Years before he trained Rocky or terrorised Gotham City, Meredith was one of the most respected actors in America, so when he invited Betty to be his guest at A Night of Stars at Madison Square Garden, she was thrilled. A suspicious Natalie wasn't keen on the idea, but as it turned out, Meredith had no designs on Betty's honour; he just wanted to make his ex jealous. In a newly bought dress, Betty spent a dreamy evening at one of New York's most glittering events, and Meredith was a consummate gentleman, content to show his date off to Paulette Goddard, his most recent ex and eventual wife. It was an intoxicating night of glamour, a tantalising taste of how the other half live, but once the band packed up and the stars went home, the princess turned back into Cinderella. At the ripe old age of 17, Betty was left to wonder if her big break would ever come.

Franklin Street

Never one to let a chance slip by, when Betty heard that casting for ingenue roles was underway for a new comedy named *Franklin Street*, she hurtled across to the Lyceum Theatre to find the director, George Kaufman, in the theatre lobby. Betty scored herself an audition and this time, callbacks followed. Before each reading, Betty worked on her lines at home with her beloved dog, Droopy, determined that this time she'd get the elusive role. Betty's home life was nurturing and loving, and Droopy and Natalie had her back in a way that would have been alien to the distant Bogarts. Natalie was there to wish Betty luck before every one of those auditions and callbacks, so imagine her delight when, after an agony of waiting, Betty Bacall was finally given the news that she had dreamed of. She'd got her first speaking role in a show that was bound for Broadway.

As *Franklin Street*'s gawky dreamer Adele Stanley, Betty would perform first in out-of-town try-outs before bringing the play to Broadway. In what seemed to be a good omen, the play would premiere the day after she turned 18. Whilst Bogie was busy on Warners' wartime pictures, playing the hero and vanquishing Nazis left, right and centre, *Franklin Street* opted for more escapist fare. Betty had been so excited to get the part that she piled an unthinkable amount of pressure on herself, determined to be perfect even at the first rehearsal. Instead, her anxiety was so acute that she could barely get her words out and when she did, her trembling voice was a whisper. Sitting around the table in the rehearsal room all she could do was compare herself unfavourably to the rest of the cast, but once she left the table and started to act, Betty's terror faded.

Eventually the cast set out from Penn Station and Natalie waved her daughter off with a reminder that she was a 'nice Jewish girl' who should always be on her guard. Betty should remember to behave herself, she warned, and to come back as good as she went off. In the role of Maud, a dreamer with a love of romantic poetry, Betty Bacall's comic timing wowed the audience from opening night. Though she would be celebrated for her poise and beauty on the screen, Betty transformed herself into a gawky nerd thanks to an unflattering wardrobe that played up her lanky physique and played down her natural grace. When the audience tittered as she made her entrance, Betty blanched. She hadn't said a funny line yet, so why were they amused? Kaufman assured her that they were laughing because she already embodied the dreamer so well: she had a gift for comedy, and that was a rare skill indeed. As it would turn out, to hear audience laughter at *Franklin Street* was an achievement in itself.

Whilst Betty revelled in the backstage bustle and camaraderie, she found her first tour a lonely experience. Though life was full when she was at the theatre, she felt adrift during the long, lonely days. Without the support system of her mother and best friends in New York, the world seemed like a very big place indeed. Despite her loneliness, though, *Franklin Street* proved one thing beyond a doubt: she really could act.

Daily rewrites gave the cast of *Franklin Street* an early clue that things weren't going to plan, but despite the flurry of new pages the laughs were few and far between. History would show that *Franklin Street* would be Betty Bacall's first and last speaking role on stage. She wouldn't tread the boards again for another 17 years and then she returned as Lauren Bacall, a bona fide star. *Franklin Street* proved to be a dead end. 'Unless life and verve can be introduced into the production, this Broadway showing will not be an auspicious one,'[4] wrote *The Billboard*'s critic, but the bell had already tolled. The play never made it to Broadway and closed in Washington after a critical mauling.

When Betty got the news, it felt like the end of everything. Though director George Kaufman hoped the play could be salvaged and re-mounted, for now everyone was out of a job. Betty was so embarrassed that she lied to her mother, telling her that the show was closing briefly for rewrites and would reopen soon. One of the few good things that she got out of it was a review that briefly gave special mention to Betty Bacall. She treasured that first review when things went wrong, just as Humphrey Bogart kept the stinging notice that had deemed him inadequate. To Bogart, it had been a smack across the chops whilst to Betty, it was a warm embrace. And just like the man who became her husband, that early failure didn't beat her. It just reminded her of how badly she needed to act.

When Betty got home to New York, she gave one of the best perfor-mances of her life convincing everyone that *Franklin Street* would soon be back. They were all taken in – or were kind enough to pretend to be – and encouraged Betty to keep auditioning, just to fill the time before the play was back on the road. Betty hit the streets all over again, knocking on doors, chasing leads and making sure everyone knew that she was looking for work. The only thing she took a break for was to catch a movie called *Casablanca* with her mother and her aunt Rosalie. Rosalie had got it bad for

Bogie, but Betty's verdict was crushingly honest: she thought Rosalie was nuts. 'He didn't give me the swoon-droops,' she shrugged. That would change.

Harper's Bazaar

Betty's luck changed when a friend of a friend arranged a meeting with Diana Vreeland, the now-legendary fashion editor of *Harper's Bazaar*. Vreeland cut a striking figure to Betty, with her backcombed helmet of black hair and dramatic red lips and nails, not to mention her influence on the world of fashion. The meeting was perfunctory and brusque, as Vreeland took Betty's chin in her hand and turned her face this way and that, before sending her for a consultation with celebrated photographer Louise Dahl-Wolfe. These were the women who discovered Bacall.

Dahl-Wolfe didn't pose her young model, but simply snapped photographs as she chatted to Betty about how she had ended up here in the first place. A trembling Betty kept on talking and Dahl-Wolfe kept on pressing the shutter release, capturing photograph after photograph of the latest young hopeful. But this young hopeful was different.

Despite all the knockbacks, Vreeland and Dahl-Wolfe saw star power. They called Betty back in and dressed her in a smart suit and kerchief, all the time telling her that she mustn't even think of changing her unique look: the look that Betty hadn't even realised she possessed. *Harper's Bazaar* was the big time and if Betty nailed this gig, then she'd finally be on her way. She could forget the Garment Center and the prettiest usher plaudits, even the soul-sapping misery of *Franklin Street*'s early bath. Yet all of that disappointment had taken its toll on the teen. Bogie's disappointments had been punctuated by successes, and life had taught him how to roll with the punches. Betty had been taught that she could do and be anything she wanted, but life seemed determined to prove that wasn't the case. All of that changed thanks to Diana Vreeland and Louise Dahl-Wolfe.

Vreeland booked Betty's first location job, which would see her in St Augustine, Florida for a pre-Christmas shoot. Natalie agreed on the proviso that Vreeland would take personal care of her daughter and ensure that she was home in good time for the festivities. It was on this trip that Betty began to see something more of the woman behind the eccentricities and learned that sometimes, one had to work with what one had.

She saw it first-hand when Vreeland got her team tickets on the last train bound for New York after the shoot wrapped, despite every carriage being full to capacity. Upon learning that the train was giving priority to servicemen, Vreeland dropped the name of the railroad president at the ticket office, and swore that he had promised that his railroad would get her pregnant daughter and her companions home to New York. That so-called pregnant daughter was the super-skinny Betty Bacall and her devoted companions were actually members of the *Harper's Bazaar* crew. Needless to say, Diana got her way. She'd promised Natalie that she'd get Betty home in time for Christmas and she did, with Betty play-acting the least convincing pregnant woman ever.

When Betty's pictures appeared in the January issue of *Harper's Bazaar*, it was a personal and professional milestone. Fan letters piled up for the still-unknown model and in reply, Diana Vreeland gave Betty her own credit in the next issue. She featured in a double-page spread alongside actresses Martha Scott and Margaret Hayes, billed as 'young actress, Betty Becall [*sic*]'. Though her name was misspelt, Betty didn't care. She was in the celebrated pages of *Harper's Bazaar*; just a month later, in March 1943, her face would be on the cover.

Betty's first magazine cover was an instantly iconic image, intended to drum up support for the American Red Cross Blood Donor Service. It showcased Betty in a sharp blue suit and sleek hat, her hair tumbling over her shoulders in glossy waves. She is leaning on the door of a Red Cross blood donor consultation room, but this isn't the fresh-faced, beaming image of a serviceman's sweetheart. Instead, Betty is an ageless archetype: she's a sultry, smouldering vamp, and the face of a new generation. It was little wonder that, once a tastemaker like Diana Vreeland had launched Betty into the world at large, Hollywood sat up and took notice.

Nobody took more notice than Hollywood power couple Howard and Nancy Hawks, *aka* Steve and Slim. He was a director, producer, and screenwriter with a host of cinematic classics to his name long before he united Bogie and Bacall as another Steve and Slim in 1944's *To Have and Have Not*. Among the films that bore the Hawks name were the hard-hitting *Scarface*, rip-roaring *Only Angels Have Wings*, and peerless comedy *Bringing Up Baby*. Hawks had a particular penchant for what became the archetype of the Hawksian woman, a tough-talking, ass-kicking, no-nonsense go-getter who is more than a match for her male counterparts. She's the cool-headed mistress of her own seductive qualities, and definitely never a wilting flower or screaming hysteric. In a world where women had stepped into traditional male roles as the men went off to fight, the Hawksian woman was a modern gal.

Hollywood is built on legend and if Hawks created some of the most memorable, Slim was the woman who created Howard Hawks. To understand the dynamic of their relationship is to understand the characters that Bogie and Bacall came to play in *To Have and Have Not*.

Steve and Slim

Born Mary Raye Gross, Nancy's rise to the top of society was worthy of Hollywood itself. After meeting film star William Powell when she was in her teens, the athletic and attractive Slim became the darling of a glittering set led by newspaper magnate and *Citizen Kane* inspiration, William Randolph Hearst. Slim was seven years Betty Bacall's senior and she lived the lifestyle that Betty dreamed of, hobnobbing with the likes of Cary Grant whilst being courted by Clark Gable. She'd even enjoyed a seemingly effortless modelling career that saw her grace the cover of *Harper's Bazaar* a handful of years before Bacall achieved the same honour.

Beautiful, cool and accomplished, Nancy had already rebuffed Gable and Ernest Hemingway before she met film director Howard Hawks, at the time married to Norma Shearer's sister, Athole. The marriage was blighted by Athole's battle with depression and she spent days shut away in her rooms, assailed by voices that she believed belonged to ghosts of the First World War. And as Athole languished, her husband left her to face her demons alone.

Howard Hawks was seemingly incapable of being faithful to any of his three wives and there's more than a touch of the movies about his first meeting with Nancy. She was dancing at fashionable Los Angeles night-spot the Clover Club with future James Bond supremo Cubby Broccoli when Howard spotted her. He watched Nancy, just as his camera later lingered on the women he committed to celluloid, and when she was free, asked her to dance. During their turn on the floor, Hawks trotted out one of the oldest lines in the playbook and asked Nancy if she wanted to be in the movies. She replied with an unequivocal no, but though Nancy had no interest in acting, Hawks would commit her facsimile to celluloid over and over again. It was the start of a relationship that created one of film noir's most iconic and beloved cornerstones.

The story of Hollywood is rich in legend and happy accidents, and the road that led Betty to Slim is one of them. It began on a fishing trip, when Ernest Hemingway and Hawks were discussing the novelist's reluctance to make the shift from prose to screenplays. Hawks told his friend that he could make a great movie from even Hemingway's worst book: *To Have and Have Not*. Released in 1937, *To Have and Have Not* tells the story of Harry Morgan, the captain of a fishing boat who tries to outrun the Depression and care for his wife and children by hosting rich men on fishing trips. When one of his clients hoodwinks him out of a massive payment, Morgan is left with no choice but to get into contraband and run black-market goods between his Florida home and Cuba. Stranded in Havana by a wealthy customer who absconds without paying, Harry finds himself drawn into a swamp of crime that ends in a lost limb and murder. Scenes of Harry struggling to make a living alternate with those of wealthy pleasure-seekers who live dissolute, carefree lives, oblivious to the degradation around them. The novel's Marxist social commentary was far from a critical smash on release, but in Hawks's hands, it would morph into a new animal altogether.

Though Hemingway was reluctant to move into screenwriting, he and Hawks worked on turning the novel into a screenplay during their ten-day fishing trip. Hemingway bet Hawks that he couldn't adapt the story as it stood, and the director knew that he was likely right, so the pair went in another direction. Instead of trying to film the apparently unfilmable, they stripped out most of the plot – and all of the Marxism – shifted the location and played up a sizzling romance between Harry Morgan and the sultry Marie Browning. Then they set the project aside.

Once the trip was over, Hemingway and Hawks went back to their own respective projects. Still disinterested in the movies, the novelist eventually sold the book right to the Hughes Tool Company, who promptly sat on the property for four years. In late 1943, Hawks bought the rights back and sold them on to Warner Bros at a huge profit, making roughly ten times the amount of money Hemingway had received, much to the author's chagrin. Business was business.

The responsibility for rewriting the screenplay was given to Jules Furthman, Oscar-nominated for 1935's *Mutiny on the Bounty*, and Hawks's co-writer on *Only Angels Have Wings*. Furthman's new screenplay preserved the Cuban setting and reintroduced much of the original novel, but Hawks once again asked for multiple revisions. Desperate to capture his wife's sultry appeal in the leading lady, some of Marie's lines were actually taken verbatim from sizzling conversations between the couple. Most notable was her infamous 'you know how to whistle' seduction, arguably Bacall's most iconic moment on film, and one that Hawks owed entirely to his wife. Ironically, given how *To Have and Have Not* played out, once Bacall was cast, the screenplay was revised again, this time to reduce her role in case she wasn't as good an actress as she was a model. In the event, Warners had little to fear. As Bogie joked, 'I have the feeling of a mouse that's going to be torn apart by a rabbit.'

The Code

When the screenplay of *To Have and Have Not* hit the desk of Joseph Breen, the man responsible for enforcing the Hays Code, he took out his red pen. Little noticed when it came into force in 1922, the Hays Code, more formally known as the Motion Picture Code, was a set of guidelines that studios were expected to apply to their output in order to make a morally palatable product. In short, it was a handy guide to self-censorship, and films that stuck to its rigid rules were awarded a certificate of approval. As the Code gained more traction, studios found it was easier to play ball rather than risk inviting more interference – potentially from the government itself – and eventually the near the knuckle pre-code material that had once thrilled audiences became nothing but a fond memory. Lovers kept one foot on the floor, married couples slept in twin beds, and everything was as clean as could be. It stayed that way until the Code's death rattle in 1968.

Joseph Breen was a devout Catholic who believed that the Hays Code was all that stood between America and moral degradation; he was appointed to the head of the Production Code Administration in 1934. For decades, Breen presided over the strictest rules that Hollywood had and would ever know. His power was unparalleled and at his word, studios would leap into action to rewrite scripts, excise scenes and bend a movie to his moral will. One of his most famous interventions came with Alfred Hitchcock's *Rebecca*, which was forced to change the powerful ending of Daphne du Maurier's novel, excising Maxim's murder of his first wife. In the book, the second Mrs de Winter lets it go, reasoning that Rebecca's bad behaviour left her husband with no other choice. For Breen, this was unthinkable: nobody could get away with murder. So *Rebecca* received a new climax, in which Rebecca's death was an accident, and her tormented husband was guilty of no more than concealing the circumstances.

Bogie had run up against Breen before when he refused to allow any explicit mention of *Casablanca*'s Ilsa and Rick having slept together. Any chance that Ilsa and Rick might get a happy ending was off the table too – it was unthinkable for a married woman to desert her heroic husband. Instead, Ilsa was forced to get on the plane with her spouse and fly out of Rick's life, leaving him to watch her go with noble fortitude. It is one of the most famous moments in movie history, and certainly contributed to *Casablanca*'s legendary status. A happy accident for Joseph Breen.

When Warner Bros received Breen's report on *To Have and Have Not*, they learned that he had identified dozens of code violations. Virtually all of these came from the original novel and included Morgan's killing a man in circumstances that weren't self-defence, multiple references to sex and the inclusion of obvious sex workers. No Hollywood leading man was about to take a role in which he lost an arm, so that element of the plot was out too, and that was only the beginning. Breen's wasn't the only voice raised in objection to the screenplay. Even the government got involved.

Upon learning that the action was set in Cuba, the Office of the Coordinator of Inter-American Affairs raised concerns that *To Have and Have Not*'s portrayal of the Cuban regime would be an embarrassing violation of the United States' Good Neighbor policy. Hawks brought in William Faulkner to work on revisions,[5] starting with a relocation to Martinique. He then addressed himself to Breen's notes and made numerous amendments in concert with Hawks, who dreamed of mimicking the success of *Casablanca*. All of this was still happening during casting and pre-production; by the time shooting began at the end of February 1944, only three dozen pages of the screenplay had been completed.

Cover Girl

But we're getting ahead of ourselves. With Hawks and Warner Bros settled on Bogie for the role of Harry Morgan, the only question Bogie had was who would play Marie Browning. When he got the answer, he was none the wiser. Humphrey Bogart, one of the biggest stars in the world, an Oscar nominee with millions of fans just waiting to part with their hard-earned cash, was going to be paired with a nobody.

Betty Bacall's big Hollywood break is a Tinseltown legend. Supposedly, Nancy and Howard Hawks were relaxing at home when Nancy picked up the new edition of *Harper's Bazaar* and was stopped in her tracks by the cover image of a sultry vamp tempting blood donors to make her day. Hawks was seeking an untried and unknown talent to nurture and mould, and Slim knew that she had found the woman her husband was searching for. She tossed *Harper's* across to Hawks and said, 'I like her face. Why not find out if she can act?' He took one look at Betty Bacall and started making calls.

In fact, that's not quite how it happened. Like all the best Hollywood legends, it's a glossed-up version of an even more one-in-a-million truth.

As Hawks told Peter Bogdanovich, far from seeing Betty splashed across the covers of *Harper's Bazaar*, Slim actually spotted her in a tiny picture in *Vogue*. It's a better story in its way, but it isn't the one that stuck.

Howard Hawks wasn't the only Hollywood name vying for the attention of the unknown model. Betty's uncle Jack, an entertainment lawyer, fielded calls from Howard Hughes, Columbia and David O. Selznick, the legendary producer of *Gone with the Wind* and *Rebecca*, which had snatched the coveted Academy Awards for Best Picture in 1939 and 1940 respectively. Betty knew nothing of the burgeoning interest until her uncle Jack sat her down and went through each offer with her, keen to proceed with caution rather than haste. Diana Vreeland encouraged Betty to sign with Columbia, who wanted her to portray a *Harper's Bazaar* model in Rita Hayworth's forthcoming movie, *Cover Girl*, alongside a number of other real-life cover stars. It might not be a featured role, but it was the sort of publicity that even *Harper's Bazaar* couldn't buy.

Of the offers from Hughes and Selznick, little more was said. After his initial enquiry, Howard Hughes fell by the wayside whilst Selznick was concerned about Bacall's similarity to K.T. Stevens, his popular recent discovery. It was a case of been there, done that, and he declined to make a solid offer. That left a choice between two: Columbia or Howard Hawks.

Uncle Jack came down in favour of Hawks. The Columbia deal offered Betty a bit part and came with a year's contract with options which could keep her in limbo if they exercised them then decided not to use her. Hawks wasn't holding out promises, but he wasn't holding out handcuffs either. Under the deal negotiated by Charles Feldman, Hawks's agent, Betty would be sent to Hollywood for a couple of months on a salary of $50 to make a screentest. If the screentest was a success, she would receive a personal contract. If not, she'd be free to look elsewhere.

It was the biggest decision of Betty's life. If she signed with Columbia, she was guaranteed no more than one film appearance. With Hawks, she might come away with nothing but a failed screentest and a few dollars, but she might come away with a contract with one of the brightest and most successful talents in Hollywood, not to mention the very real chance of a leading role. The decision was made: Betty would go with Hawks.

Though Natalie had always been her daughter's greatest champion, there was no chance that she'd be able to throw in her job and accompany Betty across the country, and there were no other candidates to act as chaperone. At 18, Betty would have to go it alone, armed only with

Charles Feldman's promise to her mother that she would be well taken care of whilst on the west coast.

Let's take stock for a moment, just as Betty must have. If it seems like she'd been slogging for years to make it, it's worth remembering that she was still only 18. Success with *Harper's Bazaar* seems to have been a long time coming because Betty had just packed so much into so short a time. She'd been a model, a stage actress, a cover girl and now, if things worked out, she'd be in the movies.

The City of Angels

Betty left New York on 3 April 1943, clutching her train ticket as she embarked on her greatest adventure. The night before, the entire family had gathered for an emotional farewell dinner and Betty took her beloved dog, Droopy, aside to explain that she would soon be home. Betty wept and waved from the window as the train departed Grand Central Station, and she left behind the life she had known forever. As she settled back into her seat, safe in the luxurious berth that marked the start of her adventure in motion pictures, the young actress took a deep breath. On the wall opposite, she watched her reflection in a mirror and told herself, 'Well, Betty Bacall, this is it.' It certainly was.

Three days after she left the bustling streets and towering skyscrapers of New York City, Betty arrived in Los Angeles. She had crossed the continent, but to Betty it felt as if she'd come to a whole new country. The sun-drenched streets were free of yellow cabs and the empty pavements were wide and flanked by palm trees on every side. It was like stepping into a movie.

From the moment she climbed down from the train, Feldman kept his promise to look after his charge. Betty was met at the station and taken directly to Feldman's Beverly Hills office where she promptly found herself bowled over by him. He was a flirt but a gentleman, and showered Betty with compliments that left her positively glowing as she settled into the Claremont Hotel for her first night in Hollywood, dreaming of the triumphs to come. It was the start of another crush.

The Brown Derby restaurant on Wilshire Boulevard is an instantly recognisable symbol of old Hollywood. The playful derby hat conjures up the Golden Age at a glance, and for Betty Bacall it was the site of a formative meeting. It was here, on 7 April, that she and Feldman slipped into a booth to await the arrival of Howard Hawks, the man who would make or break her dreams of stardom.

By the time Hawks arrived, Betty was already eaten up by nerves. Crippled by anxiety, she fell back on her tried and tested approach of saying very little, but Hawks took her silence as the same sultry insolence that had drawn him and Slim to her in the first place. Hawks and Feldman did most of the talking and a lot of it was about Betty's teeth – Feldman wanted to get them fixed, but Hawks wouldn't hear of it. Hawks asked Betty how much acting experience she'd had and she answered honestly, giving him a rundown of her training and curtailed stage career. Hawks took it all in, weighing her up as he did.

Hawks gave nothing away, merely telling Betty that he would arrange a screentest for her, before she returned to her hotel alone. Yet Betty had never been the sort of girl to sit and twiddle her thumbs, and in Los Angeles she fell back on one of her familiar routines. She visited Feldman's office every day just as she had haunted the offices of Broadway's producers and casting agents. The only difference was she was asking about her screentest rather than the chance of landing a walk-on.

On Betty's first weekend in town, Feldman invited her to his luxurious Coldwater Canyon home to have lunch with his wife, Jean Howard, and enjoy her first experience of the real Hollywood lifestyle. When Betty met the elegant Jean and settled on a terrace overlooking the couple's sprawling estates, she saw the life she wanted. She had already developed a crush on Feldman, but Betty's crushes were regular occurrences, and Jean became the latest. Betty thought the former Ziegfeld girl was one of the most glamorous creatures she'd ever seen, but she was relieved to discover that despite her closets full of silk and jewels, Jean was utterly down to earth. She offered Betty friendship, invaluable in a city where she knew nobody, and told her that anytime she needed a pal, she was to call at Coldwater Canyon.

Betty was grateful for the Feldmans' support in a lonely city. She had never learned to drive and as the days at the Claremont stretched out interminably, she decided to fix that. When she wasn't taking driving lessons, she wrote to her mother or to Betty Kalb with endless stories of Hollywood, but the anxious waiting threatened to sabotage her chances when the fabled screentest did roll round. And make no mistake, Betty wanted that screentest more than anything.

A series of lunches with Hawks seemed to suggest that it would happen soon, but even as she read scenes for him, the chance to step in front of a camera remained tantalisingly out of reach. In fact, Hawks was testing Betty all the time. Though Feldman was flirtatious and friendly, Hawks was a different sort of man altogether, deliberate and self-contained. At first he had seemed guarded but the more time Betty spent with him, the more she saw another side to the man who could make or break her. He shared stories of his adventures in Hollywood, but they were always anecdotes in which he had the last laugh; nobody bettered Howard Hawks. Betty simply didn't know how to respond to him, so when he spat a throw-away insult about a Jewish acquaintance, her blood ran cold. Suddenly an unexpected and awful possibility loomed: if Hawks was an anti-Semite and learned that she was Jewish, what would he do? Would that be the end of a promising career before it even began? Betty took her concerns to Feldman, who laughed them off as nothing but his friend's affectations.

> Of course, it was Howard Hawks who changed my life ... Despite all of his great accomplishments – *Bringing Up Baby* (1938), *Scarface* (1932), some of the best pictures to that date – his one ambition was to find a girl and invent her, to create her as his perfect woman. He was my Svengali, and I was to become, under his tutelage, this big star, and he would own me. And he would also like to get me into his bed, which, of course – horrors! It was the furthest thing from my mind. I was so frightened of him. He was the old gray fox, and he always told me stories of how he dealt with Carole Lombard and Rita Hayworth, how he tried to get them to listen to him and they didn't, so they never got the parts they should have gotten, and their careers took much longer to take off.[6]

What Betty didn't realise at the time but would much later, when she knew a little bit more about the reality of Hollywood, was that Howard Hawks was positioning himself to be a Svengali. She was the ideal blank canvas on which he could paint his perfect Hawksian woman, recreating his wife up on the silver screen for all the world to see, but placing her totally in his control. He would dictate everything, from how she wore her hair to how she was presented and who she would speak to, and he would remove any agency she might hope to possess. Betty was to be made in the image Hawks demanded and, he hoped, she would become his lover too.

Beginnings

After weeks of inaction, the Hollywood machine suddenly cranked into life and Betty was summoned to the Warner Bros lot for make-up tests. She was placed in the hands of make-up supremo Perc Westmore, another man who would attempt to create his own version of Betty. He decided to pluck Betty's brows, alter her hairline, straighten her teeth and craft her into an American version of Marlene Dietrich. His plans sent a panicked Betty scurrying to complain to Hawks, who immediately slammed on the brakes. Hawks told Westmore that there was to be no American Dietrich: he wanted Betty exactly as she was, crooked teeth and unplucked brows. Westmore did sneak a pair of unobtrusive false eyelashes onto the unwilling actress, but in all other respects he obeyed. Betty left the chair wearing a light, natural look that was barely there by 1940's standards.

With that panic quelled, Betty learned that her test would consist of a multi-page scene from *Claudia*, played opposite fellow young hopeful and eventual TV star Charles Drake. She spent the night before the screentest that would change her life forever in a guest bedroom at the Feldmans' house, literally sick with nerves. The stakes seemed almost impossibly high.

When Bogie arrived in Hollywood, he was already a seasoned actor who had learned to roll with the punches life threw his way. Not so Betty, who, for all her sullen and vampy looks and whirlwind New York days, had seen little of the world. Bogie had grown up and grown hard on the family battlefield: Hollywood wasn't a dream factory for him, but a place to make some money and meet a few drinking buddies. For Betty, it was a sugar-coated wonderland.

As an usher, Betty had grabbed quick hellos backstage with actors, but at Warner Bros she was sitting in the make-up chair alongside the likes of Ann Sheridan and eating lunch in the commissary a few tables away from Errol Flynn, before heading to the Feldmans' to party with Cole Porter. Betty wasn't their equal yet, but as wide-eyed and starstruck as she was, she knew that she was taking the smallest of steps into the world of the Hollywood dream factory. And all the time, with every flick of the make-up brush or sweep of the hairstylist's comb, her anxiety was gnawing.

The conditions of Betty's screentest were a testament to the belief Hawks had in his new protégé. Hollywood cranked out dozens of tests every single day, perfunctory affairs done with little ceremony, but Hawks gave Betty the star treatment. The eight hours she spent at the lot that day gave her just a taste of the future that could be hers, from the best make-up artists in the business to her own stand-in and carefully tailored lighting. It was unheard of for an unknown's screentest and Betty was thrilled when she told her mother, 'Everyone told me that what I had only one out of 10,000 girls gets.'[7] But Hawks had a lot to lose – he'd staked his reputation as a Svengali on success.

As he watched the test, Hawks made his mind up almost immediately: Betty Bacall became the first woman he had ever signed to a personal contract. Her new life in Hollywood had begun. The contract would need to be approved in court due to her age, but that was just a formality. When Natalie agreed to bring Droopy and join her daughter on the west coast in a new apartment at 275 South Reeves Drive, it all felt real for the first time.

As Betty celebrated, Hawks was still scheming, determined to stage-manage every aspect of her debut. There would be no press and no glittering parties, because he wanted to keep his Trilby under wraps just a little longer, so she could make the biggest impact imaginable. And he loved being in control. Betty's low-key debut actually came when her minor contract was approved in court and a photograph appeared in the press, but she didn't make the headlines. Yet.

With the paperwork filed, Hawks set about refining Betty Bacall into the star he wanted her to be. In a Hollywood bursting with Betties, he would choose her name just as he had chosen her wardrobe, hair and make-up. He even chose her voice. Betty already spoke in a low register, but whenever she got excited, her voice shot up in pitch. Hawks hated this girlish instinct: he wanted a smoky smoulder and set her to work achieving it. To speed up the process and with her driving licence now secured, Betty got into her newly purchased old car and motored out on Mulholland Drive. Once she had reached a secluded spot, she sat overlooking the canyon and read books aloud, all the time concentrating on keeping her voice low. Of course, by the time this story made it into the movie magazines, the truth had been massaged into something rather more befitting of Hollywood.

> She is about to be publicized by Hollywood as 'the girl who shouted her way to fame' but don't you believe it ... The 'shouting' idea is another press agent's dream.
>
> The story goes that once Lauren Bacall had come to Hollywood – and she did so at the invitation of director Howard Hawks, whose wife had spotted her face in an American fashion magazine – Hawks told her to go out for a couple of hours a day and shout across the canyons which split up the Hollywood hills.
>
> It isn't exactly true but it sounds well and it's safe to say that if she would have done it nobody would have called the police, because in Hollywood hills much stranger things happen the clock around.[8]

Betty's first official publicity shots, by John Engstead, were taken in Hawks's Bel-Air home on Moraga Drive. Here she met Slim, the woman who had started it all, and marvelled at the couple's opulent mansion. This time it was Slim who took control. She had already picked out some of her own outfits for Betty, whose first shoot under contract to Howard Hawks went like a dream. Now all that was left was to put her in a movie.

To Have and Have Not

Growing up in New York had made Betty impatient. She was born and raised in a city where nobody waited around and where, when something was supposed to happen, it did. In comparison, the pace of life in the City of Angels seemed almost absurdly leisurely. Still not 20, Betty felt as though she had no time to lose and eagerly waited to see what Hawks had planned for her. She wasn't used to doing nothing; she wanted to be in front of a camera yesterday, not in a week or a month or who knew how long.

In fact, six months passed without any screenplay being delivered to Betty's door. She continued with her voice practice, reading for Hawks periodically and receiving a masterclass in the Hawksian woman. The director asked her to adopt what he regarded as a more masculine approach to performance; simply put, he wanted her to be insolent. 'That was the only way you noticed her,' he observed, 'Because she could do it with a grin.'[9] She took the note and, for six long months, concentrated on doing just that.

Though Betty relished the moments when Hawks or Feldman introduced her to the most dazzling stars, it was just a reminder of everything that lay tantalisingly out of reach. Occasionally the two men would make some throwaway comment to remind Betty that Hawks was mulling things over, even going so far as to say that he'd like to put her opposite one of two men: Cary Grant or Humphrey Bogart. At the mention of the debonaire Bristolian, Betty's heart soared. Grant was a megastar who had worked with Hawks previously to great acclaim. He was also regarded as one of the most handsome and charming men in Hollywood... just the sort of chap that a girl like Betty would love to work with. When it came to Bogie, the jury was out. Where Cary Grant was tailored and suave, Bogart was rumpled and weathered. Next to the Englishman, he was ten miles of dirt road.

What Betty didn't know was that Hawks had made Bogie a very telling promise. Whilst shooting the breeze over future projects, Hawks told the actor, 'I think you are the most insolent man on the screen. In your next picture I'm going to try to make a girl more insolent than you are.'[10] Not find, not discover, but make: Svengali never sleeps. Bogart reminded Hawks that he'd had decades to become so effortlessly insolent, but Hawks was up for the challenge. 'Every scene you play together,' he said, 'she's going to walk out on you and leave you with egg on your face.' And Bogie loved the idea. All that was left was to find the girl.

In a world at war, albeit one that was seeing the tide of battle turn in favour of the Allies, Hollywood had wised up to what audiences wanted. Flag-waving patriotism was the flavour of the hour: heroes who triumphed against the odds overseas and loyal gals who kept the home fires burning were literally singing America's praises in the biggest movies of the year. Although *Casablanca* loomed large in the list of box office big hitters at the end of 1943, the runaway hit was its Warner Bros stablemate, *This Is the Army*, also helmed by Michael Curtiz. A musical comedy featuring a score by Ray Heindorf and lyrics by Irving Berlin, it starred future POTUS Ronald Reagan, and would remain the highest-grossing musical of all time until *White Christmas* snatched its crown more than a decade later. Many of 1943's top spots were taken by musicals, alongside such inspirational fayre as *The Song of Bernadette*, and the heavier wartime drama of *For Whom the Bell Tolls*, another Hemingway adaptation. Hollywood had correctly anticipated and effortlessly dictated the direction of wartime entertainment, moulding its content to perfection for a public whose sons were going off to fight. The days of prohibition and Scarface were gone, but the Nazis and fifth columnists and their heroic resistance fighter foes still had a little life left in them. The studios were going to wring every last drop out of the common enemy.

For Betty Bacall in 1943, the war was something that happened to other people. It wasn't that she didn't care, but her eight months in Hollywood had left precious little time to keep up with the news. Instead, as the year drew to a close, she could boast a contract with Howard Hawks and a diary that included parties with the likes of Bing Crosby and Robert Montgomery, who dismissed Betty as 'too easy' when she handed over her telephone number as soon as he asked for it. What he mistook for over-eagerness was actually Betty's sheltered upbringing showing itself – to Betty, it simply seemed impolite to refuse. All that the teen couldn't boast – yet – was a movie role.

As the year drew to a close, Hawks mentioned to Betty that he was working on *To Have and Have Not*. Betty had never heard of the book, though of course she was familiar with Hemingway... who wasn't? Hawks told her that the film would star Humphrey Bogart, currently shooting *Passage to Marseille*, and he invited his protégé to visit the set and meet the leading man. Betty was used to being introduced to stars by now; Bogie was no big deal.

If this was a Hollywood movie, that first meeting would be fated to go one of two ways. Heavenly choirs of angels would sing, a radiant sun would shine and Bogie and Betty would fall in love at first sight, dazzled by their soulmate. The other possibility has been fuelling romcoms for years. There'd be a meet cute, before mutual loathing gradually gave way to love, helped along by a series of comical mishaps. Legends have sprung up of snippy exchanges and long, sizzling looks, but there were no angels and no pratfalls, and definitely no smouldering glances. Disappointingly, it was just a polite introduction between one of the biggest stars on the planet and the 19-year-old hopeful who dreamed of joining him in that feted pantheon. The meeting was nothing to write home about, but a quick hello and a little small talk with Bogart, who was as polite but reserved as ever around anyone who wasn't one of his drinking buddies. After all, Mayo didn't need any more ammunition.

Bogart left the US to visit troops in Casablanca soon after Christmas, but before he departed, he watched Betty's screentest and okayed her for *To Have and Have Not*. His easy acquiescence to Betty's casting shouldn't pass without comment. As an established star and one of the biggest earners in Hollywood, Bogie could have vetoed the decision to cast an unknown as his leading lady if he had wished. The fact that he didn't suggests that he still remembered his own early days in Hollywood, when he was a struggling no-name desperate for a break. There was one last obstacle to overcome. With Hawks's backing, Betty wasn't exactly out on her own, but she still had to impress Jack Warner with a second test. This time, the scene would be lifted straight out of the nascent screenplay of *To Have and Have Not*.

Betty didn't think too much about her meeting with Bogie until a few days later, when Hawks finally gave her the news that she had been desperate to hear. He had found the perfect vehicle to launch his new protégé: *To Have and Have Not*. The very first scene Betty read was the one that made her famous and stuck with her to her dying day, the famed, sultry 'whistle' sequence. The now-legendary dialogue was nowhere to be found in the novel, because it came straight from Hawks's wife, the real

Slim. But *To Have and Have Not*'s Slim was fictional: Hawks could control his wife at last.

> Slim: You don't have to act with me, Steve. You don't have to say anything and you don't have to do anything. Not a thing. Oh, maybe just whistle. You know how to whistle, don't you, Steve? You just put your lips together, and blow.

Betty had read a dozen pages for her screentest but now everything would hinge on one scene, which she would perform with actor John Ridgely. She got to work, spending every waking moment studying her lines and ensuring that she truly embodied the character of Marie, *aka* Slim. Every single day she and Ridgely met up to rehearse and every single day Betty had to perch in the actor's lap and kiss him. For a young woman who had never had a boyfriend and who found even a photographer's lens nerve-racking, it was a true baptism of fire.

Despite her daily rehearsals in Howard Hawks's office, Betty rarely glimpsed anything of the real Svengali beneath his carefully constructed public persona. He was deliberate, considered and remote, a far cry from his colleague Feldman, who was every bit as friendly, carefree and encouraging as Hawks was saturnine. Hawks protected himself even as he re-shaped Betty, never consulting her in the process of her recreation. He had set out to make a star and ultimately it was he who would have the final say when it came to Betty Bacall's as yet non-existent movie career. His wisdom was rarely shared, though he did give Betty one piece of direction that he considered was the secret to bringing Slim to life: whatever else Betty did, she must focus on that sultry insolence that Hawks found so attractive. As Betty herself wondered, 'Who knew what kind of Frankenstein's monster he was creating?'[11]

Betty and John Ridgely shot the scene exactly as Hawks had directed. Behind the camera was Sidney Hickox, who would go on to work as cinematographer on *To Have and Have Not*, and who understood instinctively the noirish look that Howard Hawks wanted. Betty felt as though the test was a success, but she wouldn't know for sure until she got a chance to see it a few days later alongside Hawks and Jules Furthman, by then deep into the job of writing *To Have and Have Not*'s screenplay. Betty arrived at the studio brimming with confidence, but when she watched the screentest in the darkened projection room, a creeping horror left her sick with fear: she was dreadful. As the realisation that she'd blown it crept through her body, an embarrassed Betty slid down in her seat and waited for the scene to run through the projector, dreading the moment when the lights went up and her fate was decided. Betty Bacall's Hollywood dream would end in a Warner Bros projection room, with a disaster of a screentest that would slam the door in her face forever.

As light flooded the room and the reel reached its conclusion, Betty braced herself for the bad news. She was her own worst critic and this time she couldn't have been more wrong, because the usually saturnine Hawks delightedly revealed that he'd already shown the test to Jack Warner, who loved it. With Warner's seal of approval, the wheels started grinding at last: Betty would star as Marie opposite Humphrey Bogart in *To Have and Have Not*. The only condition Jack Warner insisted on was that Hawks sell 50 per cent of his starlet's contract to the studio, but it was a price the Svengali was happy to pay. When Bogie bumped into Betty a few weeks later, he told his leading lady, 'We're going to have a lot of fun together.' History would certainly prove that to be true.

So now Betty had the look, the voice and the movie role, but she was still lacking the all-important movie-star name. Oh, sure, Bacall had the requisite glamour and hints of the vampishly exotic, but Betty? Betty was the girl who made apple pie and danced with the boy next door on prom night, she wasn't the sultry, mysterious siren whom Hawks had dreamed of. Instead, she'd be billed as Lauren Bacall, a name befitting a star. Hawks instructed Betty to tell the press that the name had been her great-grandmother's . . . it was the kind of lie Hollywood was founded on. From now on, Betty's life would be rewritten, adding a suggestion of blue blood that didn't sit too well with the family she had left behind in Manhattan. But Hollywood was a long way from New York.

Betty knew that a starring role opposite Humphrey Bogart was the sort of debut that money couldn't buy. It was certainly the sort of debut that few could dream of making. However, Betty had never understood the sex-symbol appeal of Bogie – to be fair, neither did he – and she later told a journalist, 'I wasn't at first wild about the idea of working with him. I expected a tough, overbearing, opinionated, crude, ill-mannered and ill-educated man . . . He turned out to be not quite so bad as that.'[12]

The Look

Before we leave Betty's Bacall's story behind and dive into the maelstrom that was *To Have and Have Not* and the early days of the relationship, we can't forget The Look. The Look became Lauren Bacall's signature, a vampish, smoky-eyed gaze from beneath Betty's eyelashes that burned out of the screen like a flame. Yet the famed, celebrated look was no creation of Hawks, nor was it a deliberate ploy to play up the sex-kitten image of the smouldering Slim. In fact, The Look came about by accident, and totally out of necessity.

When Betty's first day on set rolled around, her nerves were utterly overwhelming. She arrived to find Bogie and Mayo already waiting and a welcoming Bogie introduced the two women, no doubt painfully aware that his wife would soon be already spinning all sorts of wildly jealous fantasies about the starlet. For Bogie it was business as usual, but for Betty it was nerve-racking, a hundred times worse than the fashion shoots that had left her paralysed with self-conscious anxiety. Mayo's narrow-eyed glare did nothing to help.

Intending to ease Betty into the business of making movies, Hawks had decided that she would shoot just a single scene that day. In it, she would have a short exchange with Bogie, catch a box of matches that he threw to her, then light a cigarette. So far so good, until Betty walked out on set shaking so violently that the camera caught every tremble. Bogie was no diva and did his best to settle her nerves, but still the close-up was going to be a challenge. On the plus side, Mayo's consuming fears about her husband's leading ladies evaporated once she realised just how innocent Bacall really was. As far as Mayo was concerned, the threat to her marriage would come from an established star who was well-versed in the arts of glamour and seduction, not some trembling teenage ingenue.

And the shaking really was going to be a problem. It was only once Hawks had called action that Betty discovered a way to keep her trembling head in check. She tucked her chin down as low as it would go, until it was almost touching her chest, then peered up at her co-star from beneath her eyelashes. Mission accomplished. Hawks watched unimpressed, doubtful that it would be enough to carry her through the picture and convince audiences that she was a sultry, self-possessed siren. But it seemed to work. Even better, it sizzled. The trembling ceased and Lauren Bacall morphed from a nervous, gawky teenager, helpless in the grip of terror, into a purring vamp. The Look was born.

Act Three

Bogie and Baby

Slim: I'm hard to get, Steve. All you have to do is ask me.
Steve: You know what you're getting into. It's gonna be rough.

Hump and Betty

There are many ugly stories in Hollywood that feature powerful men and hopeful women. Too many to count, in fact. This is not one of them. The love story between Humphrey Bogart and Lauren Bacall surprised them as much as anyone else.

Humphrey Bogart was never starry. He wasn't a prima donna, nor did he wield his celebrity to the detriment of others. The very fact that he was happy to star opposite the unknown Bacall on the strength of a couple of screentests and an unremarkable chat on the set of *Passage to Marseille* speaks to his willingness to give someone else the break that he had chased for so many years. He knew that the new starlet on the scene would be a great publicity angle for the studio and would likely do no harm to the box office. Yet there were plenty of big-name leading ladies who would have given *To Have and Have Not* just as much publicity, not to mention more punch at the ticket booths. Nor did Bogie say yes to assuage his bosses or because he liked the idea of a pretty young co-star; he said yes because he was Bogie, and when he believed something was right, he stuck with it.

Lauren Bacall couldn't have asked for a better baptism into the ways of Hollywood. As deliberate in his filmmaking as he had been in creating his starlet, each morning Hawks would gather his stars on set and go through that day's scene with them beat by beat. They would work on blocking and tinker with lines, going through the daily rewrites that were intended to up the sex and smoulder quotient. When they weren't working, Bogie and Betty cycled all over the lot together or joked around like old friends, pranking and fooling as though they'd been buddies for years. Bogie was known for his acerbic sense of humour but he softened it for Betty, because he wanted to put her at ease and keep the movie on track. Hawks watched their burgeoning relationship with growing concern and not a

67

little jealousy. Perhaps he could see what was slowly unfolding on set, even if everyone else was oblivious to it.

Bacall and Bogart were both born in New York City and both ended up on the call sheet for *To Have and Have Not*, but that seemed to be all that they had in common. A quarter of a century and two very different lives divided them, but there's often more to love than shared past experiences. Opposites attract might be a cliché, but it's proven true on more than one memorable romantic occasion. And Betty had expected a very different sort of Bogie: people often did. Like the men who approached him in bars looking to start a fight, including those who ended up on the wrong side of Mayo's hot temper and sharp stiletto heel, Betty had been sucked in by a screen persona. There was a scrappy side to Bogie, but there had to be: he might have been raised in privilege, but he had never fit into that gilded world. Bogie was an outsider from the off, and he never compromised on that. In today's parlance we might call him authentic, but that word could have been invented for Humphrey Bogart. For better or worse, he was authentic to his last breath.

Yet the screen version of Bogie, that grizzled, hard-bitten, cynical bruiser with a hidden glimmer of romance, was not entirely a construct. He might have dodged physical altercations with his challengers, but life had left him hard-bitten. He had taken the knocks and kept on pushing, and it was written in every line on his face. After two failed marriages and one marked by violence and melodrama, whether he had any romance left in him was debatable. He still sought refuge with Helen Menken when-ever things at home got too bad, but he always came back to Mayo and Sluggy Hollow.

There was a sensitivity about Bogie that surprised Betty, especially when it came to those crippling nerves of hers. On set he did everything he could to put her at ease, but it was all strictly down the line; there was no flirtation, no trying it on and no unwanted attention. The paths that had led the two to that Warner Bros soundstage in April 1944 might have been very different, but the thing that eventually united them wasn't seductive glances or good looks, it wasn't even smooth talk; instead it was a shared sense of humour. Despite the quarter century that lay between them and the totally different lives that they lived away from the camera, Bogie and Bacall could make each other laugh, and the more they laughed, the more at home Betty felt. She fell in love easily, or thought she did, and her crushes on older men piled up one after the other without seeing any reciprocation, but Bogie didn't join that laundry list of idle dreams. Instead, perhaps to Betty's surprise, he was becoming her friend.

The Kiss

Having moved out to Los Angeles to support her daughter, Natalie had found that life on the west coast didn't suit her nearly as much as it did her little girl. She'd got to know the Feldmans and Hawks and was reassured that Betty would be well cared for, which meant she was free to return to New York and the family and friends she missed so much. Besides, she would still be there on the end of the telephone or at the mailbox, posting letters to her daughter and reading those she received by return. It was in these letters that Betty breathlessly summed up her feelings about Humphrey Bogart.

> Everything is working out beautifully for me. Howard told Charlie the rushes were sensational. He's really very thrilled with them ... Bogie has been a dream man. We have the most wonderful times together. I'm insane about him. We kid around – he's always gagging – trying to break me up and is very, very fond of me.[1]

Perhaps the kiss was inevitable. Three weeks into the shoot, when filming had almost wrapped for the day. Betty was at her dressing table combing her hair. As she waited to be called for her final shot, Bogie strolled into the dressing room to wish his co-star goodnight and the couple were soon kidding around. It was then that Bogie made his move. He didn't pounce on Betty, nor make a lunge, but instead touched his fingertips beneath her chin and kissed her. Just like that, one of Hollywood's most celebrated love affairs began. Despite knowing that Bogie was married to a wife with a fearsome reputation, when he asked Betty to scribble her number on the back of a matchbook, she didn't hesitate. Bogie pocketed the matchbook and left Betty to shoot her scene and ponder on what had just happened. Her mind was reeling.

How are we to view this moment that changed lives and wrote Hollywood history? Betty went home in an excited fog, whilst Bogie went home to Mayo, but he took with him a killer secret in their unwinnable game of one-upmanship. Mayo's jealousy and suspicion was out of control, and now she really had something to be jealous of, she had absolutely no idea. Is it a stretch to imagine that Bogie relished this particular secret, especially in a marriage that seemed to allow no secrets whatsoever? The Battling Bogarts made their explosive arguments public, and they took no prisoners. They tore up hotels and restaurants, dragging bystanders into their fights, and they left friends and dinner guests reeling as insults, food and even impromptu weapons went flying. Mayo had been on the set to check out the new ingenue in town and, watching Bacall shake and stutter her way through her first scenes, dismissed her as an amateur. She feared the worldly-wise actresses of Hollywood who had money, prestige and power; the nervous, trembling teenage girl was no threat to her what-soever.

Mayo, whose jealousy was a thing to behold, didn't know her husband nearly as well as she thought she did. Or if she did, she had underestimated the competition. Bogie might disappear in search of sanctuary with Helen Menken on the east coast, or sink into the oblivion afforded by his circle of boozy mates on the west, but in Bacall he had found something different. He little knew it when he kissed her that night, but he had found the One.

Bacall, on the other hand, had not lived the life that her would-be paramour had known. She had not watched her love affairs and marriages crumble and, truth be told, she'd scarcely seen much of life at all. Instead, Betty had nurtured one unrequited crush after another, most of them on older men. She was a hopeless romantic, always swept up in the idea of an idyllic love affair without ever having to deal with the harsh realities that came with one. Sometimes it's hard to remember that she was only 19 when she met Bogie, given just how much she'd done in that relatively short life. She'd been a *Harper's Bazaar* cover sensation and the leading lady in a Bogart movie, handpicked by Howard Hawks himself, and she spent her off time gadding about Hollywood parties with superstars... it's little wonder that she was in a romantic fug, living out her very own Hollywood dream.

When Bogie and Bacall talked on the phone that night, they kept up the romantic fiction. Just like in the movie, she called him Steve – later the name they gave their son – and he called her Slim. 'I hate "Lauren",' Bogie told *Photoplay* once their romance was a matter of public record. 'I never did like it.'[2] Like so much in Hollywood, it barely seemed real, but they both knew they had to keep it low-key on set. None of this was new to Bogart, a man of the world who already had three marriages and countless other relationships. For Betty, it was one more Hollywood experience.

Secrets

The affair – for it was an affair, even if it wasn't yet sexually intimate – played itself out with as much discretion as the couple could manage. Not quite enough discretion, if Hedda Hopper's warning to Bacall of 'Better be careful. You might have a lamp dropped on you one day,' is anything to go by. But Betty was never afraid of Mayo for herself, only for what she might do to Bogie. Whenever Bogie was out with Betty, friends assured Mayo that he was dining out with 'the cast'. The couple took lunch together and talked on the phone late into the night whenever Sluggy was otherwise engaged, and Bogart told his new paramour that old story: his marriage had been a mistake. But the one thing he never asked for was pity, nor did he make any promises; he was married, and that was that.

For all their efforts to keep their relationship hidden, a movie set is like a family and secrets are hard to conceal. The intimacy between the two leads was obvious to the always perceptive Howard Hawks and he called Betty to a meeting at his home, where he warned her off. This wasn't some great love, he assured her, but a flirtation, the simple and unavoidable by-product of working together in close quarters and shooting intimate scenes. Once the movie wrapped, that would be that; Betty would be jettisoned as damaged goods by Bogie and the industry alike, and her middle-aged Romeo would cruise back to Mayo, leaving her to make trash for Monogram. He couched it as concern but it was plain old jealousy; Bogie had got the girl he'd earmarked for himself.

Bogie was furious at the director's meddling. Hawks was mad because he wanted – no, needed – to be in total control. Betty had been entirely at his beck and call and now, with Bogie in the frame and her confidence increasing, he'd lost that control. She was starting to think for herself. Ironically, in trying to warn Betty off Bogie, Hawks had pushed them closer together than ever. In many ways, all those threats of Poverty Row only spurred Betty forward. In urging her to forget Bogie, he drove her straight into his arms.

In Hollywood, Betty Bacall had felt lonely and lost, despite the star-studded parties where Hawks paraded his latest discovery. In his marriage to Mayo, Bogart was just as lonely. Betty fell for his unexpected vulner-ability and the gentle and sensitive nature that was at odds with his tough guy persona. He fell not only for her beauty, but for her bold, unaffected attitude and quick wit, and her belief that she could do anything she wanted. Betty craved the opportunity to learn from Bogart, a respected, instinctive actor with decades of experience under his belt, and he craved the opportunity to become her mentor and protector. This was not the age-old story of an older man swooping on a younger woman, it was a genuine rapport.

71

Bogie and Betty's romance soon heated up, though it remained relatively chaste. They worked out ways to be alone, leaving the studio in their own cars and meeting on secluded streets to exchange kisses or hold hands and talk about their hopes and dreams. There is something curiously naïve about all of this, but Bogie was just as inexperienced in the ways of courting as Bacall. Her excuse was youth, his was the constant, intense hunger that he brought to every endeavour, whether it was his career or his love life. He had scrapped all his life for every break, and pursued every success with a dogged intensity, but in those stolen meetings he could taste just a little bit of innocent courtship.

Svengali

There was nothing innocent about Betty's feelings. Despite her vampish image she was completely inexperienced, but admitted when she was a little older and more self-possessed that her sexual attraction to the worldly older actor had been so intense that it was a pure gut reaction. She confided the affair to her friend, Carolyn Cromwell, who was also seeing a married man. It was a shared secret that the two women could discuss openly in a world where such things were never to be mentioned. But Betty's adoration of Bogie began to bubble over into everyday life, until he was her only topic of conversation. No doubt some shrugged it off as a teenage crush or a passing fancy, but for Betty, Bogie represented so much that had been missing. And she did just the same for him. Despite her youth, Betty offered love and nurture, whilst he was the father figure that Betty had never had. She reflected, 'All the love that had been stored inside of me all my life for an invisible father, for a man. I could finally think of allowing it to pour over this man and fill his life with laughter, warmth, joy.'[3]

It's ridiculous to try to pretend that a lasting romance with Bogart wouldn't have material and professional benefits for Betty, but for a young, beautiful, up-and-coming actress with the backing of Howard Hawks, there would be plenty of romantic candidates who didn't come complete with two divorces and a violently jealous wife. Lauren Bacall seemed to be everything that Bogie had been searching for in his marriages: a loving, nurturing companion who shared his values and dreams. She embodied the sort of warm devotion that had, until now, escaped him, but she wasn't the gingham-clad housewife that he had pined for. He was older, worldly wise and weary with experience, but when Hawks discovered the affair, Bogie crumbled, seized by the inescapable sense that he had failed. On set he was Betty's mentor, sharing with her the secrets of performance, whilst off set he was her romantic suitor, promising friendship, affection and protection. Yet despite all of that, all that he thought he could give her, Hawks's dark threats of career oblivion drove home just how little protection Bogie could really offer.

When Hawks threatened to wreck her nascent career, Betty was devastated, not for her work, but because she feared her secret romance was on the verge of collapse. Aware now that Hawks's ego wouldn't allow him to be rejected, she swore that she'd keep things professional from now on. When Natalie visited from New York and found out what had been going on, she hit the roof; Hawks and Feldman had promised to protect Betty and instead they'd let her run wild. The truth came tumbling out when Bogie called Bacall late at night after a drunken row with Mayo and asked her to come out and meet him. Betty bounded out of bed and into her clothes, then flew off to comfort her unlikely Romeo. Seeing her daughter jump to answer the summons, Natalie insisted that the couple cool it. The sight of her little girl running after a married drunk like a well-trained lapdog left her furious. Natalie had given her daughter a model example of independent womanhood and had taught her never to let herself be taken advantage of, but Bogart, who commanded all the professional power and influence in the relationship, seemed to be doing exactly that. And Betty was letting him. Faced with her mother and Hawks's shared ire, the sophisticated star-in-the-making reverted back to being Betty Bacal. Bogie might have nicknamed Betty Baby, but she had been Natalie's baby first. Betty swore to both Hawks and Natalie that she and Bogart were over, before they had even really begun.

Bogie's response was to fall back on the one thing that had never let him down: the bottle. He started drinking with more fervour than ever and became increasingly oblivious to his own wellbeing, both physical and mental. After an incident in which Bogie tried to prove his toughness by biting a chunk out of a wineglass and chewing the shards, cutting his mouth to ribbons, it seemed as though he had tipped over the edge into self-destruction. He blamed himself for the dimming of Betty's Hollywood dreams and the guilt was crushing. Because of him, Hawks had Betty balanced on the edge of a precipice with Monogram at the bottom. Bogie had imagined himself as a protector of this innocent damsel against the wolves of Hollywood, but instead he was the one who had put her in their sights. Upon learning of her lover's distress, Betty flew back to his side once more. They resumed their after-dark liaisons in secluded cars and stole lunch dates by inviting a friend along to keep up the façade of respectability. It was only a matter of time before Mayo found out.

Suspicion

'Hello, lover boy. How're you doing with your daughter? She's half your age, you know.' When Mayo snarled at Bogart down a phoneline on the Warners' lot, it must have felt like a bullet in the gut. Shooting on *To Have and Have Not* was coming to an end and with it went Betty and Bogie's ironclad excuse to keep canoodling. He pulled the plug: the romance was too hot to handle with Mayo on the prowl. Emotions as Hawks called cut for the final time were mixed, as jubilation at the sense of having wrapped what felt like a special picture jostled with sadness at the end of the affair. A heartbroken Betty mooned over the man who had got away until Bogie reignited the romance with a letter that, in keeping with that hidden, romantic side of himself, he signed Steve.

> I wish with all my heart that things were different – someday soon they will be. And now I know what was meant by 'To say goodbye is to die a little' – because when I walked away from you that last time and saw you standing there so darling I did die a little in my heart.

The split couldn't and didn't last and before long, the affair was back on. With her friend Carolyn in the passenger seat, Betty would make the two-hour drive to Balboa by night to meet Bogie as he served with the Coast Guard in support of the war effort. He had an hour free during his shift and he spent it with Baby, whilst Carolyn was left to entertain herself. Then the women would head home, a return journey of another two hours. Yet despite his promises to protect Betty, Bogie made no effort to untangle himself from Mayo. Betty didn't believe in marriage and never expected them to last, so the state of her lover's relationship was simply more evidence that she was right. Though Bogie nobly told himself that he didn't want to hurt either woman, it was inevitable that someone would suffer in the end.

'Baby, I do love you so dearly and I never, never want to hurt you or bring any unhappiness to you,' Bogart wrote as he wrestled with his conscience and options.

> I want you to have the loveliest life any mortal ever had. It's been so long, darling, since I've cared so deeply for anyone that I just don't know what to do or say. I can only say that I've searched my heart

thoroughly these past two weeks and I know that I deeply adore you and I know that I've got to have you.

They were fine words, but they came with a caveat: Mayo Methot. Bogie's other marriages had ended almost by default, when husband and wife went off to pursue their respective lives and careers, but Mayo had given up everything that wasn't Bogie or booze. She had become Bogart's wife and drinking partner, his bitterest enemy and most fierce defender, and the homemaker who looked after their house and pets when she was sober enough to do so. Mayo would not let her husband go so easily.

But Bogie was in love, and deeply so. In his letter pledging himself to Lauren Bacall, he wrote, 'Baby, I never believed that I could love anyone again, for so many things have happened in my life to me that I was afraid to love – I didn't want to love because it hurts so when you do.' It might sound like the trite sentiment of a man who doesn't know what he wants until he gets it, but Humphrey Bogart was being honest. He really did adore Lauren Bacall, yet he was a man from another era and that genteel, emotionally sterile upbringing had left its mark.

As summer rolled on, a stolen hour here and there morphed into longer meetings at Betty's place, where a visiting Natalie graciously agreed to give the couple the occasional afternoon to themselves. Quite something, considering her lingering righteous fury. 'I want to make a new life with you,' Bogie wrote. 'You'll soon be here, Baby, and when you come you'll bring everything that's important to me in this world with you.' It seems likely that the affair was consummated in the summer of 1944, when Bogie walked out on Mayo after a violent argument in the early hours of the weekend. He trudged miles along the highway in a rainstorm and Betty raced out into the storm to find her lover, eventually picking him up in the middle of nowhere an hour out of Los Angeles. They spent what remained of the weekend together in a borrowed trailer. From that point on, there was no turning back.

The couple began to take risks, never more so than the August of 1944, when Bogie and Betty made plans to spend a few days together in Newport on a borrowed boat. Mayo was expected to be in town and Bogart would keep his wife occupied until his lover had been safely smuggled aboard the boat. Upon her arrival, Betty learned that Mayo had broken her foot in a drunken accident, so she was stuck at home. Safe in the knowledge that they wouldn't be interrupted, Betty and Bogie played house; he even took her to the yacht club where she sat uneasily amongst the Bogarts' social set.

It established a pattern that became more and more common as the year moved towards its close; Bogie began to introduce Betty to his friends, who inevitably found themselves roped in to conceal the romance, supplying boats and trailers, cars and alibis. They were frequently called upon to play third wheel at dinner and lend the rendezvous a façade of respectability. And the more it went on, the more frightened Betty became of what Mayo would do to Bogie if they were discovered.

The Battling Bogarts

Imagine, then, how much that terror was magnified the next day when Betty and Bogie were canoodling on their borrowed yacht, only to hear Bogie's friends bellowing a warning that Mayo was on her way. In a blind panic, Bogie bundled Betty into the loo and dashed ashore to intercept his wife. Betty huddled in the tiny bathroom, silent and terrified until her lover and his wife finally drove away and she could escape. As she fled from the marina, Betty must have reflected on the contrast between her glamorous Hollywood lifestyle and an afternoon spent hiding in a toilet. It was hardly the A-list. But Mayo's impromptu appearance proved one thing – she knew something was up. And once she was suspicious, she wouldn't rest.

Despite the passionate intensity of Bogie's feelings towards Betty, whether sexual, emotional, or intellectual, he remained conscious of his commitment to the disintegrating Mayo. He wanted to leave and Betty was willing to wait, but he couldn't bring himself to humiliate his wife. After all, the revelation that he had been cheating on her with his 19-year-old co-star would be indignity enough; there was no way that Mayo could escape hurt, but the last thing Bogie wanted was to see her suffer.

Mayo's suspicions ate away at her until she made Bogie a desperate promise to give up the booze and straighten out, if only he stuck around. Concerned for Mayo's fate if he walked out on her, Bogie agonised over his decision. He believed that he owed Mayo a debt for all she had done to build their home after giving up her own career, and after six years of marriage, Bogie couldn't bear to cut her off. Just before Lauren Bacall's twentieth birthday and shortly before *To Have and Have Not* was due to open after knockout previews, Bogie told her that he had to try to save his marriage. He was from a different place and time, where men squared their shoulders and sometimes turned their back on the thing they wanted most of all. And so it went until a large bouquet of flowers arrived out of the blue. The card was addressed to Steve, from Slim.

A few days after her birthday, Betty received word from New York that her grandmother had died. The unhappy news opened the floodgates and grief overwhelmed her. She had lost her lover, then her grandmother in quick succession, and the sorrow washed away any excitement she might have felt as she looked forward to the release of her first movie. Betty met Bogie only once during their latest separation, when they accidentally ran into one another on Warners' lot. The meeting was short, friendly and centred mostly on Betty's new car; it was the only topic that felt even vaguely safe.

Basking in the glory of the preview audience feedback, Warners immediately announced that they would reunite Hawks, Bogie, and Bacall, as soon as they could. The day after the announcement, Hawks bought the rights to Raymond Chandler's *The Big Sleep*. The news should have been another triumph for Bacall and Bogie but instead they were miserable, hiding the pain of their broken romance beneath a veil of strained, agonising friendship. The thought of sharing another movie set was unbearable.

To Have and Have Not opened in October 1944, six months after shooting had wrapped. Today the film is lauded as a solid-gold classic and remembered as the spark that ignited the flame under Bogie and Betty. At the time, critics were not so favourable. Reaction from the press was mixed at best, with the picture dismissed as a poor successor to *Casablanca* that ripped up Hemingway's original source material in favour of romantic derring-do. Ultimately the element that most interested critics was Lauren Bacall, the unknown cover girl with the devastating look. Yet none of the critical sniffiness bothered the box office, where the movie was soon raking in receipts that came within a whisker of the stellar business *Casablanca* had done around the world.

SHE has been described by critics and others as 'an American Dietrich' – 'a tall Veronica Lake' and 'what most men expect their favourite girl to look like' … She has no mink coat or any furs. She dwells with her mother in Beverly Hills … Her approach (on the screen) to a male is similar to the technique used on women by men, rues and ordinary everyday wolves. She plays a 'wolverine.'

Lauren attributes some of her success to what she calls her 'down-under look.' A sort of bashful glance upward with the head slightly bowed. It was natural with her a year ago. Now it is a habit which she practices on newspapermen.[4]

Bogart was already a superstar, but *To Have and Have Not* catapulted him to the top of the Warners' slate, where he became their most bankable name. For Bacall, the film was the turning point that launched her blazing into the Hollywood firmament. The unknown New Yorker more than held her own against her seasoned leading man, smouldering when they flirted and sultry when she sang to the accompaniment of Hoagy Carmichael. As playwright Moss Hart told her dryly, 'from here on you have nowhere to go but down'. Sitting as she was on top of the world, as she and Bogie resumed their affair, Betty brushed away his warning. She little knew how right he was.

The Big Sleep

What should have been a triumph for Bogie was marred by more trouble at home. Mayo was jealous even when there was nothing to be jealous of but now, with her husband disappearing on the lamest excuses, she just knew. She forgot her promises and started drinking and lashing out, leaving Bogie to respond in kind. Things had always been volatile between the couple but they could usually be relied upon to drift back together. Now, for the first time since he married Mayo, Bogie could see a glimmer of something fresh and unspoiled: there was the chance of a new start for a man who believed the world had long since run out of surprises. *The Big Sleep* started shooting on 10 October 1944; within a week, the Battling Bogarts were back in the press.

HOLLYWOOD, Oct 19—
The battling Bogarts have fought the main event. It resulted in their separation. Humphrey Bogart, $200,000-a-year screen bad man, admitted today. Mrs. Bogart, the former Mayo Methot, was not available for comment.

'Sluggy is at home,' said Bogart. 'I moved out.'

Bogart always called his wife Sluggy. He explained, with the candor [*sic*] for which he is noted, that he called her Sluggy because 'she slugged me so often.' ... Mayo gave up acting when she became Mrs. Bogart.

He said today, through a press agent, that he really had nothing to say except that he and his wife had a little talk and decided to separate. And, 'I believe the public will realize that this is of deep concern to us and will respect our wishes in not wanting to discuss it.' That is a typical Hollywood separation statement.[5]

But beneath that typical Hollywood separation statement and Bogart's joke that 'I live dangerously – both in pictures and out,' lay a dark truth. Having abandoned her career for marriage and become ever more dependent on alcohol, Mayo was in a spiral of self-destruction. Bogie was going down with her, and Betty was clinging to him like a rock. Once again Natalie balked and once again Howard Hawks tried to put the brakes on, but it had gone too far for that. Hawks vented his fury on his protégé, thundering that 'Bogart likes his life – he likes the drinking and he likes his wife – you're throwing away a whole career because of something that's just not going to happen!' but Betty wouldn't be moved. She no longer needed a Svengali, and at 20 years old was certain that she knew her own mind. What she hadn't counted on was that old-fashioned something that formed the very core of Humphrey Bogart.

Faced with Mayo's declining health and fearing for her life and sanity, Bogart went back to his wife. 'I had to go back,' he told Betty. 'I wouldn't throw a dog out in the street in her condition. I have to give her every chance.' As Betty wept, the couple were pictured in the press celebrating their reconciliation in photographs that are as awkward as they are contrived. Like a million other celebrity couples who tried to paper over the fissures, they are pictured smiling and intimate, but all too often in the centre of the pictures is the ever-present glass of booze.

There was no chance that the Bogart marriage could ever be happy, yet still the couple ploughed on, and every time they fought, broke up and reconciled, the foundations crumbled just that little bit more. On screen, Bogie was the epitome of male strength: a hard-talking, hard-drinking, grittily romantic anti-hero. Off screen, he was falling apart. He was drinking more than ever, battling Mayo at home and Hawks on set, and trying to convince Betty that he could be there for her, whilst failing to convince himself that she wouldn't drop his baggage as soon as she realised how much he carried. He loved her, he wanted her, but he was sure that he would destroy her. The Bogie baggage was heavy indeed.

Bogie and Bacall's romance had been fresh, invigorating and thrilling on *To Have and Have Not*. On *The Big Sleep*, things had turned toxic between Bogie and the jealous Hawks. Worst of all, it showed on set and on camera. It showed too in Bogie's scenes with Betty, who was buckling under the strain. The Bogarts split again in early December and Bogie moved into the Beverly Hills Hotel alone, whilst issuing a statement that denied the involvement of any third party. It was at the Beverly Hills Hotel that Bogie and Betty's affair blazed back into life with a vengeance.

With Carolyn as her decoy, Betty made secret visits to her lover, sneaking up back stairs and through kitchens, and hiding in the closet whenever room service arrived. Once upon a time, nobody would've had a clue who she was, but she had lost the cloak of anonymity forever.

When Mayo promised to enter rehab, her desperation went straight to her husband's heart. Bogie blamed himself for his wife's lost career and dependency on booze, and he vowed to stick by her until they could make a mutual, sober decision about their future. He broke the news to Betty as they waited for the cameras to roll. The timing was terrible. As the crew waited, the toast of Hollywood was sitting in the bathroom, frantically pressing ice to her swollen eyes, desperate to recover her composure enough to shoot her scenes. If that was bad, things got worse when a drunken Mayo intercepted a late-night phone call between her paralytic husband and Betty. She snatched the phone from Bogie and began berating her rival, screaming, 'Listen, you Jewish bitch – who's going to wash his socks? Are you? Are you going to take care of him?' It was just days since Mayo had left rehab; supposedly back on track, she had started drinking again almost immediately. There was more than a grain of truth in her rueful admission to a newspaper that 'I just want him. It's become a habit to love Bogey [*sic*] and it's hard to break it.'[6]

Separation

Christmas proved to be Bogie's breaking point. He had been drinking more or less constantly since his reconciliation with Mayo and had finally fallen off the cliff edge. When he failed to show up for work after the Christmas holidays, Warner emissaries were sent to collect the star. They found a shell of a man, physically and mentally unable to do his job. Always the pro, Bogie tried and failed to get back to work; he even managed the odd day before he was drunk and collapsing again. In all his life, with all his troubles, Bogie had never before held up a movie, and Hawks could see *The Big Sleep* slipping through his fingers. What a director could do without his leading man was limited, but Bogart was too far gone to care. The only person Hawks could put pressure on was Lauren Bacall. And he did.

Hawks had already tried and failed to break the couple up, but faced with the turmoil on set, he threw everything he had at ending the affair. He told Betty that Bogie was too old for her, reminding her that she was nothing but a plaything to punctuate the fights with Mayo, the woman he truly loved. Bogie had nothing to lose in romancing a young, glamorous co-star, but it could cost Betty everything. Would she really risk her entire future for a man who would throw her aside sooner or later and to run back to his wife? Betty wept as Hawks railed against her, swearing that he would never have signed her if he'd known what would happen, and telling her again and again that he could destroy her at a stroke. In the end he did nothing of the sort, and instead sold his remaining share in her contract to Warners for a million dollars: Hawks was tricky, but he wasn't stupid. The sale freed Betty from his influence, but proved a bitter reminder of an actor's powerlessness in the face of the studio system. They were effectively commodities to be bought and sold.

But no threat could have worked, because Betty was starry-eyed with love for Bogie. He occupied her every thought and she ached to be with him, to support him in his trials. At 20 years old and drunk on dreams of a future with the man she loved, she had made her choice. It was her naivety that Hawks had ably exploited when he threatened her with Poverty Row. When bullying failed, he turned to matchmaking instead.

If Betty had a thing for older men, Hawks had just the candidate to take her mind off Bogie. He and Slim invited her to dinner at their place, promising, 'I've got the most dazzling man you'll ever meet in your life for a fourth – once you meet him, you'll forget all about Bogart.' That dazzling man was none other than Rhett Butler himself. Immaculate in his military uniform, Clark Gable was about as far from Humphrey Bogart as a man could get. He was charm personified and seemed to exist on a rarefied plane of glamour and effortless Hollywood style, but Betty was unmoved. She loved Bogie not in spite of the rumpled air of world-weariness that suggested a man who needed to be nurtured, but because of it; assured, confidant and suave, Clark Gable was doing just fine without her. Hawks wasn't using to losing, but he had lost his grip on Lauren Bacall. 'You know Bogey [*sic*] didn't fall in love with you. He fell in love with the part. You've got to play it all your life,' Hawks warned as his influence dissolved. 'She said, "I will." And she did. Now, there's a girl the camera liked.'[7]

The Big Sleep is rich with knockout performances from its female cast. Martha Vickers's performance was eventually significantly reduced thanks to her consistently overpowering Betty, but perhaps the biggest takeaway is Dorothy Malone, who left a lasting impression in her role as a worldly and flirtatious bookstore clerk. Malone had been signed to RKO at the age of 18 and despite appearing in several blink-and-miss-them roles, she had made little impact. That all changed with *The Big Sleep*. At the 1957 Academy Awards, Malone would win an Oscar for her knockout performance opposite Betty Bacall in *Written on the Wind*.

But Hawks wasn't the only one with doubts. Natalie echoed his warnings that Betty was on the verge of throwing away everything for a hopeless crush. After all, just how often did the Bogarts need to split up and reconcile before Betty accepted that they were always going to find their way back to each other? As one journalist wryly put it, 'Bogart and his wife … resolved to make up so they could break up right some day.'[8] That day had come. When Bogie returned to work on *The Big Sleep*, his mind was made up. He and Mayo had finally had the talk and made their decision: it was over.

The couple's final separation coincided with the end of shooting on *The Big Sleep*. The shoot had been a long way from the romantic excitement of *To Have and Have Not*, eventually staggering in a month late and $50,000 over budget; Bogart's spiral had been costly in all sorts of ways. Yet when the picture wrapped, he was ready to press ahead with a divorce. Bogie moved back to the place he started: the Garden of Allah, and tried to rebuild his shattered health and life. The marriage to Mayo had wrung the couple out.

> I have always wanted a career … But I have also always wanted a home of my own, a husband and children. I made up my mind long ago, that when I did find them they would come first. If my career interferes with our domestic life, it's best that I give it up.[9]

It wasn't only Bogie who had choices to make. Betty wanted her career, but she was ready to give it all up to be a wife to Bogie, and he was ready to make a commitment. Mayo had finally accepted that the time had come to put a full stop on her marriage, and asked for a settlement that included more than half of Bogie's cash assets along with a clutch of valuable investments. Her husband was willing to agree to anything to buy his freedom. That night he dined with Mary Philips, the second ex-Mrs Bogart, and confessed that his relief was tempered with sadness. It might be the right thing to do, but it marked the end of another failed dream.

Divorce

The answer was a Reno divorce. This peculiar quirk of American law allowed couples to divorce in six weeks if one of them had been resident in Reno, Nevada, for the same unbroken period. It took a lot of convincing, but in return for her settlement, Mayo eventually agreed to go to Reno in March and stay there for the required six weeks so the divorce could be swiftly finalised. Whilst she was away, Bogie would take a trip to Malabar

Farm in Ohio as a guest of his friend, Louis Bromfield, and Betty would be making a tour of personal appearances. It was a sensitive time, but to prove his commitment, Bogie commissioned a ring for Betty from high-class jeweller John Gershgorn. In return, Betty gave Bogie a little bronze rabbit. It was a reference to her invisible but constant presence in his life, just like that of the rabbit in the play, *Harvey*.

The next time they saw each other would be in February 1945, on a promotional tour for *To Have and Have Not*, by which time Betty had been officially promoted to star status by Warner Bros. Mindful that Mayo must remain in Reno if the divorce was to be finalised, Bogie and Betty agreed to show discretion in order to spare her any additional pain. The fact that Sluggy the dog had been renamed Slim was a sign that this time, the separation wouldn't be resolved with a kiss and a drunken fist fight.

Marriage was on Bogie's mind already, but Betty didn't see any need to rush the legalities. She wanted to be with Bogie, but had little faith in the institution of marriage. Instead, she tried to convince her lover that he could take his time, having been through three failed marriages already. Besides, he still had a wife, albeit one who was in Reno. Bogie wasn't having any of it. 'Please fence me in Baby,' he wrote. 'The world's too big out here and I don't like it without you.'

All Mayo had to do was wait out her six weeks in Reno, but the mercurial Mrs Bogart simply couldn't stay the distance. After a fortnight, she wandered back to Los Angeles and stayed there for forty-eight hours. Her unexpected return had reset the clock. Now she had to restart her six-week stay in Reno from the beginning, or the hoped-for quickie divorce would be delayed again and again. It was a tense time.

Reunited

As Bogie and Betty, or Baby, as he called her, were reunited in New York to run the publicity gamut for *To Have and Have Not*, Bogie was ruminating on the enormous changes that his life had undergone since he first laid eyes on Lauren Bacall. He had wrestled with their age difference, with what the gossips would say, with Natalie, with Howard Hawks, but most of all with Mayo, and when he hit rock bottom, Betty had been willing to risk everything to stand by him. Neither would back down now. Betty didn't believe in marriage and Bogie's romantic history was bitter proof that it didn't work, but when he proposed, she accepted. The couple even began to think about kids as Betty found herself swept along with Bogie. It seemed like a crazy sort of dream.

Bogie had ridden the merry-go-round of love and marriage three times already and knew all too well how quickly it could turn into a roller-coaster. For Betty, this was her first love affair and it was all the more potent for that. She had enjoyed the occasional date and entertained some pretty major crushes, but never before had a man fallen in love with her. Bogie was in his 40s, grizzled and cynical and in the grip of a booze habit that Jack Warner memorably said 'could dissolve all the paint on the set'. Betty was twenty-five years his junior, possessed of an idealism born of youth, and she had fallen into her Hollywood dreams at the first attempt. She had never known the grinding struggle that Bogie had endured and he knew – just knew – that she'd walk away once she really got to know him. Despite all of this, he was willing to take a chance and so was she. If it lasted, it would be a miracle; if it didn't, at least they could say they tried.

> [My father] gave nothing. Somewhere, unconsciously, that must have affected my feelings about men, my basic distrust of a relationship with a man being able to last any length of time. I thought if a relationship lasted for five years it was a miracle.[10]

'I felt deserted by my father,' Betty admitted, and she had been. 'We all grow up with scars, and that scarred me when I was very young.' William Perske was nothing but a memory, a distant figure who lingered indistinct on the edge of her existence. For most of Betty's life, he had shown no interest in his daughter, but as she scaled the heights of fame, Perske couldn't help but glimpse her face on newsstands and movie screens. Suddenly the man who had wanted nothing to do with his daughter decided that she would benefit from some fatherly advice. And he issued it as a statement in the press.

> Lauren is far too young to marry a man more than twice her age. But she's a girl with a mind of her own, and the chances are that she will marry Bogart. If the wedding happens, it sure won't be with my approval. My daughter's studio advised me to keep my trap closed, but I just felt like opening it.

William Perske's reappearance in Betty's life left his daughter in turmoil and her mother furious. Still he pressed on, giving interviews and playing the part of the supportive, loving father. But against the Warners' publicity machine, his shouting was a whisper. William Perske's daughter had got on just fine without him or his name for two decades, and what he thought of the marriage proved to be of little interest to anybody.

When Betty arrived in New York that February to begin a promotional tour, she was accompanied by Natalie and Droopy the dog, by now father to Puddle, another of the many pets upon whom Betty and Bogie would dote. The trio were greeted at Grand Central Station by a mob of press and photographers and the only topic of conversation was her romance with Bogart. All too aware that Mayo still had to see out her stint in Reno, Betty handled their questions with cool aplomb. She assured the press pack that she hadn't seen Bogie in weeks and that there were no wedding plans, little knowing that Bogie and his booze habit were working hard to undo all the discretion they had shown so far. As Betty played it cool, a drunken Bogie was propping up the bars of Manhattan and telling friends that he was pining for Baby. It was only a matter of time before the secret got out.

The last time Betty Bacall had been to the Gotham Hotel in Manhattan, she was a tongue-tied youngster, awestruck at meeting Bette Davis. Not even a dozen years later, she was the star in the plush suite, the face on the cover of *Life* magazine who the press were clamouring for. The sultry vamp's notorious Look had bewitched the world. What none of them knew was that beneath that insolent beauty there lay an overwhelmed innocent, pushed headfirst into the limelight overnight. Betty exuded cool self-possession when she faced the press at the Gotham, but inside she was desperate to escape the cameras and hurry to Humphrey Bogart's suite for their longed-for reunion.

As soon as Betty arrived, Bogie started calling. He rang half a dozen times an hour, filled with a righteous fury about the parade of journalists and press agents that Warners had lined up to see his girl. Yet that wasn't what really lay at the heart of his annoyance. In reality, he was a bundle of anxiety, absolutely sure that Betty must have seen the light during his absence and decided to end their relationship. He had his suspicions that he might have scuppered it himself, thanks to a boozy night on the town in Cleveland with journalist Norman Siegel. Bogie had got drunk again and the liquor had loosened his tongue, leading to the sort of scoop that was gold dust to gossip columnists. A whole week before Betty, her mother and Droopy left for New York, Bogie had spilled the beans.

> Humphrey Bogart, bad man of the movies whose wife is suing him for divorce, today confirmed reports of a romance with Lauren Bacall, budding screen actress.

Bogart, resting at the Mansfield, Ohio, farm of author Louis Bromfield, told columnist Norman Siegel of the Cleveland Press that the
romance was 'very definite.'

'I expect to see her in New York during the next two weeks,' Bogart
said. 'Lauren is coming east with her mother and I want her to meet
my gang back there.'[11]

And every single journalist had noticed the ring Betty was wearing. The
romance was the worst-kept romance in Hollywood, but with every
passing minute, Bogie became ever more convinced that Baby had come
to her senses. Either that or Warners, Hawks and Natalie had turned the
screws and convinced her that she could do a lot better than a guy with
three broken marriages and an alcohol problem.

Bogie couldn't have been more wrong. When the couple were finally
reunited at the hotel, their future was decided. Betty was already wearing
Bogie's ring, but he took it off her hand and placed it solemnly on her
engagement finger, sealing the deal. He had had enough of pretending
and wanted to go public with dinner at Manhattan's upscale 21 Club that
night. It would be a direct acknowledgement of the romance, but Betty
didn't want her extended family to see her new fiancé in the papers before
they'd met him in the flesh, so he dutifully went along to her suite to say
hello. That first meeting was a little awkward, particularly when Bogie
met Charlie and Jack, the protective uncles who had been Betty's father
figures. He was older than both of them, but they were at least willing to
give him a chance. Somebody had to.

Bogie and Betty's romance had started with an impulsive stolen kiss in
her dressing room, but they'd somehow made it. Bogie had been through
hell, some of it of his own making, whilst Betty knew virtually nothing of
romance. She didn't trust marriage and he was sure she'd leave him, but
after the battles with Mayo and his self-destructive spiral to the bottom,
even a few years of happiness with his Baby would have been enough.
Bogie needed it, and he was ready to tell the world.

This is Humphrey Bogart Week in New York, and even the presence
of his girl, Lauren Bacall, and such headliners as Errol Flynn, Ann
Sheridan, Jack Benny, Bob Hope, Myrna Loy, Greta Garbo, Robert
Montgomery, Barbara Stanwyck, and Pat O'Brien cannot steal the
headlines from Bogie.

Mr. Bogart is currently touring the night-spots muttering to
reporters: 'I'm in love again – at my age. Did you ever meet Baby?

Betty and Bogie make it official. (*Modern Screen*)

Bogie. (*Public domain*)   Betty. (*Public domain*)

The wedding party. Bogie, Betty, George Hawkins, Louis Bromfield, Natalie Weinstein-Bacal,
Mary Appleton Wood Bromfield, Judge Herbert S. Schettler. (*Modern Screen*)

Bogie and Betty on their wedding day at Malabar Farm. (*Modern Screen*)

The Bogart family, photographed less than a year before Bogie's death. (*Modern Screen*)

Helen Menken, the first Mrs Bogart.
(*Shadowland*)

Mary Philips, the second Mrs Bogart.
(*Public domain*)

Mayo Methot (the third Mrs Bogart), and their dogs. (*Public domain*)

Maud Humphrey,
Bogie's mother.
(*Public domain*)

The Big Sleep. (*New Movies:
The National Board of Review
Magazine*)

Mayo and Bogie toast a
short-lived reconciliation
with a glass of milk.
(*Photoplay*)

Bogie and Betty.
(*Photoplay*)

Despite her best efforts, Betty never shared Bogie's love of the ocean. (*Screenland*)

Bogie, Betty, and Steve. (*Screenland*)

Louis Bromfield greets the happy couple ahead of their marriage at Malabar Farm, his family home in Ohio. (*Modern Screen*)

Bogie and Betty play farm at Malabar. (*Modern Screen*)

Mayo and Bogie bear it without the grin.
(*Picturegoer*)

To Have and Have Not.
(*Screenland*)

Betty and former would-be flame Kirk Douglas, in *Young Man with a Horn.*
(*Modern Screen*)

The Bogarts at sea.
(*Photoplay*)

Mayo signs her final
divorce papers.
(*Modern Screen*)

Howard Hawks and the stars he unwittingly – and unwillingly – brought together. (*Photoplay*)

Betty, Bogie and others prepare to attend the House Un-American Activities Committee in Washington DC. (*Creative Commons Attribution 4.0 International License, via UCLA*)

The Battling Bogarts share a peaceful interlude during a trip to Naples to entertain troops in 1943. (*Signal Corps Archive*)

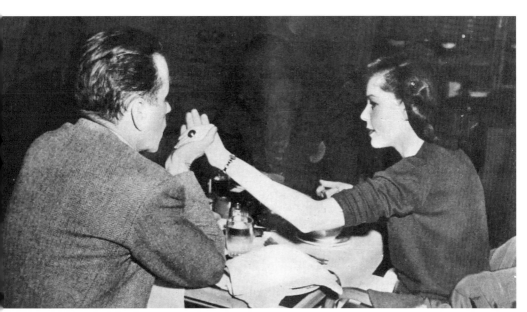

The Big Sleep. (*Photoplay*)

The Bogarts and Natalie leave All Saints Episcopal Church after Bogie's memorial.

The Bogart-Bacalls. (*Screenland*)

[Snapshots of Miss Bacall are then produced.] She's a joey. Yeah, I call her Baby and Betty. Her name's Lauren, but I call her Baby. I'm in love again!'[12]

Malabar

After years as 50 per cent of the Battling Bogarts sideshow, everything had changed. Forever. Bogie and Betty were official and she proudly showed off a charm bracelet Bogie had given her, from which hung a gold whistle. It was engraved with the words 'if you want anything, just whistle'. Everything was going to plan; Mayo was still in Reno and *To Have and Have Not* was flying high. Mayo and Bogie had left their friends reeling when fights broke out, sending roast dinners and glasses flying, but what had initially been an outrageous distraction had long since become a cesspool. The couple were an embarrassing liability, and Bogie was determined to prove to Betty that things could be different. He introduced her to his buddies and Betty swallowed her nerves and threw herself into the new social set that opened its arms to her. Even Helen Menken and Mary Philips, Bogie's first two wives, welcomed her stabilising influence. For the public, it was a Hollywood love story writ large.

Bogie and Bacall were as close to a real-life Cinderella story as anybody could imagine. Age differences in Hollywood were nothing new, nor were romances between leading men and starlets, but for the couple to be so public and so accepted so quickly was something else. What had started as an affair had blossomed into one of the most celebrated love stories that Hollywood had ever known.

Warners, however, had a different take on it. The studio system was not one that rewarded performers who wanted to do things on their own terms. If one hoped to make it in 1940s Hollywood, one had to be contracted to a studio. It was a deal with the devil, and one that many of the biggest stars of the Golden Age of movies rebelled against. Bogie had already been suspended by Warners for refusing to cooperate, and now he had gone rogue again. He watched with dismay as Betty scurried to perform every duty Warners asked of her, pulled from all sides and always in the full glare of the spotlight, and it left him furious. When an exhausted Betty refused to go on a press trip to Washington, Jack Warner sent a wire warning her to comply or else; she caved. Bogie went along too, but it wouldn't be her last tussle with Jack Warner; luckily, Bogie knew how to navigate the choppiest waters of the star system.

Warner Bros, of course, balked at the always-bullish Bogie helping their new young starlet to navigate anything. Their leading man might have been drunk when he spilled the beans on his relationship, but in doing so he had defied studio plans to stage-manage the reveal. Stars weren't supposed to seize control of their own story. Bogie's slip-up provoked a wire from the studio chastising him for his conduct, so he fired off a reply asking if they'd like him to head home to Los Angeles and help them handle Errol Flynn's publicity instead. With their golden boy facing charges of statutory rape not so long ago, Bogie's words struck home. Warners didn't bother to reply.

The studio might have slapped their leading man on the wrist, but they still knew how to win the advantage. Once the genie was out of the bottle, they turned it into ticket sales and hard cash. The interest in the couple's romance burned with white-hot intensity and wherever they went, they were followed. Eventually, Bogie and Betty were driven to sneaking out of the hotel's side door in the early hours of the morning, just so they could spend some time alone together in the fresh air.

When the publicity junket paused for breath, Bogie knew just the place to go to escape the fray. He had long loved the peace offered by Malabar Farm, the home of Louis Bromfield, and it had always been a sanctuary to him in troubled times. Pulitzer Prize-winning novelist Bromfield was a household name across America, and his works were snapped up by Hollywood as soon as they hit the shelves. Elegant, wealthy and ridiculously well-connected, Bromfield had exchanged a glamorous life in Paris for the farmlands of Ohio. When he first saw Malabar, just outside Mansfield, it was a derelict lost cause, but Bromfield fell in love. By 1945, Malabar had been nurtured into a jewel in the state's agricultural crown, where Hollywood A-listers came to till the land and feel the dirt beneath their fingernails.

Bromfield, a friend of Bogie's from his earliest days in the theatre, lived with his family in rustic Ohio splendour, surrounded by antique French furniture and happy dogs. It was the sort of domestic bliss that Bogie had dreamed of and though he loved Malabar, Mayo hadn't been so keen. She'd even trashed the place once, launching a salvo of violence that left one of Bromfield's most treasured antique lamps in smithereens. Now Mayo was gone, Bogie had once again begun to see Malabar as the sanctuary it used to be, and he wanted Betty to love it too. So, with Natalie, who would herself remarry a few years later, coming along as a chaperone, the couple paid a visit to Ohio.

Malabar Farm was the perfect location from which to start a new chapter. It was as far as one could get from the wild nights Mayo and Bogie had scrapped through in Hollywood, and might as well be on another planet to the glitzy bars and drinking dens that had been their battlegrounds. Here in peaceful, snowy Ohio, where cosy fireplaces made for a welcoming spot to relax, everything seemed simple and down to earth, if with a liberal sprinkling of antique luxury to complete the picture. America was looking forward to a future without war, to new beginnings and new hopes, and at Malabar the future and the past combined to create a heady and idyllic world. With locally grown food in plentiful supply there was no sign of rationing, and the paparazzi's lenses might have been a million miles away. It was a place to heal.

Bogie loved Bromfield like a brother and Betty was quick to follow his lead. Before long, she and Bogie came to realise that the house in Ohio would be the perfect wedding venue. The 600-acre farm offered the couple the chance to enjoy an intimate ceremony, surrounded by their closest friends and family. For two people whose lives were lived in the spotlight, it was a welcome dose of sanity and clean air. Betty in particular found herself caught up in the rural life, dreaming of a farmhouse of her own where she could play at being the perfect American housewife.

Betty wanted to become the sort of bride Doris Day played in the movies, bottling ketchup in the basement as her man went out to work. She longed to be a mother to Bogie's children, to keep house and to cook dinner. She was desperate to fit in with his friends and for her family to accept him, and she didn't want anything to get in the way. But there was work to do and whilst Bogie was about to start shooting *The Two Mrs Carrolls*, Betty was slated to take the female lead in *Confidential Agent*. Yet even as her career soared, she was considering leaving it behind.

Bogie blamed conflicting career demands for the failure of his first two marriages, but he couldn't blame divorce number three on that, because Mayo had given up acting when she became his wife. Yet he and Betty did discuss the possible price that she might have to pay. 'I agreed to put my career second, because he wouldn't marry me otherwise,' she recalled more than fifty years later. 'He said, "If you want a career more than anything, I will do everything I can to help you, and I will send you on your way, but I will not marry you ..." I made the deal, and I stuck to it, and I'm damn glad that I did.'[13] As we'll see, Betty did make sacrifices when she became Mrs Bogart, but when it came to her career, Bogie realised that it meant as much to her as it ever did. He never reminded her of the promise she had made.

Despite the whirlwind romance, the breathless reports of Betty and Bogie's love story hid a darker truth, a truth that his marriage to Mayo had been a part of. Humphrey Bogart and alcohol were a heady and unpredictable mix, even though he tried to control if during the affair with Betty. Only when they were apart did he drain bottle after bottle, glass after glass, and succumb to the drunken fog that swamped his marriage to Mayo. Now he could be with Betty openly, she glimpsed his hidden torment. After a pleasant evening at the yacht club, Betty and a drunken Bogie had their first argument. It wasn't the mutual combat he was so used to with Mayo, but a one-way flow of anger and vitriol directed straight at Betty. Bogie exploded, yelling at her and thumping his fists into the table as she tried to keep calm despite her instinct to run. Eventually it was Bogie who left, storming out into the night and leaving her alone.

When Bogie returned in the early hours of the following morning, he was sober and sorry. In his drunken confusion, he had reverted to the usual script that he and Mayo had played out so many times. He swore that it would never happen again, and was true to his word to the day of his death.

A Wedding

As the publicity machine cranked on its ceaseless way, Lauren Bacall was being hyped as the biggest thing on the planet. In early February, *Variety* reported that some radio stations had refused to air a commercial for *To Have and Have Not* because its content – namely a wolf whistle and some purple prose lauding the charms of its female lead – strayed too close to bad taste. It was just the sort of publicity that Warners wanted, and while Betty was being sold as a sultry vamp on one hand, on the other the studio was trumpeting the real-life romance at the heart of the movie. Since her father walked out, Betty remembered, 'I always dreamed of all these wonderful fairy tales, those wonderful stories of when the prince comes along, saves you and all.'[14] Bogie was an odd sort of Prince Charming.

The war was coming to an end and America's mood was jubilant. Bogie and Betty's love story was just the kind of thing that audiences were looking for, and the studio started spinning. All too aware that the alternate narrative to that same love story was a tale of alcoholism, violence and an extramarital affair, Warners instead encouraged the idea of a Cinderella tale, as much for Bogie as for Betty. Mayo simply didn't feature.

> Simultaneously with the news from Las Vegas that Mayo's divorce had gone through came a request from Chicago that [Humphrey] attend the 'I am an American Day' celebration. Turning to Lauren, with whom he was dining, he said 'Meet me in Chicago. I've got a job to do there. Then we'll go on to Louis Bromfield's and get married. Might as well kill two birds with one stone.'[15]

Humphrey Bogart and Mayo Methot were divorced on 10 May 1945. Mayo left Hollywood for New York, where she attempted to reignite her stage career without any success. She could often be glimpsed back on the west coast with her latest beau, supposedly 'a fellow whose yacht was moored near the Bogarts' at Newport Beach. Mayo and Lauren Bacall would sit on deck and glare at each other',[16] but her health was already failing. Despite rumours that another marriage was imminent, Mayo slipped further into alcoholism and depression.

Bogie and Betty, meanwhile, were planning a private wedding. Time was short since Bogie was needed on set, but the couple could spare a long weekend to tie the knot. Even Natalie, who had been so disapproving back at the start of the affair, had warmed to her prospective son-in-law, along with the rest of Betty's fiercely protective family. Bogie had finally let them get to know the man Betty had fallen in love with.

Before Betty and Bogie had parted earlier that year, he had given her a ring by John Gershgorn and now the couple returned to Gershgorn to pick out their wedding bands. Despite her protestations that marriage should be taken with a whole bucket of salt and the decision to substitute cherish for obey in the wedding vows, there were some traditions that Betty wouldn't dream of abandoning. She even satisfied the need for something old, something new, something borrowed, and something blue. Despite what Bogie mirthfully told his friends, the something old was not him.

Betty bought a brown silk scarf and a suit of pale-pink wool, beneath which she would wear a blue slip with her name embroidered on it. That was something new and something blue taken care of; something old was fulfilled by a treasured bracelet, whilst something borrowed was a hand-kerchief that belonged to her mother. In the days leading up to the wedding, the couple were giddy with anticipation, playing Tony Martin's 'Mrs Me' on a perpetual loop and enjoying the trappings of married life already. They had even picked out a home on Kings Road in the Holly-wood Hills, where they would live as man and wife; Betty termed it her 'honeymoon house'. The Bogarts would eventually settle at 232 South Mapleton Drive, where they became the leader and den mother of the Holmby Hills Rat Pack.

Warners pulled out all the stops to publicise the marriage. Jack Warner shrewdly handed Betty the keys to the black Buick convertible with red leather upholstery that she had driven in *The Big Sleep* by way of a wedding gift. Bogie took one look at the interior and ordered a custom copy for his own car; Warners didn't foot that bill. Though the studio had once feared that the affair and the age difference between the key players would be a public relations disaster, it was proving to be anything but. Bogie and Betty only went along with the studio's blaze of publicity because they knew that the wedding itself, which was being organised by Bromfield's manager, George Hawkins, would be conducted in absolute privacy.

Hawkins took care of all the administration for the forthcoming ceremony with minimal fuss. He arranged the necessary blood tests as demanded by US law, booked security to stand guard at Malabar and even convinced Judge Herbert S. Schettler of the Mansfield Municipal Court to waive the obligatory five-day wait for a marriage licence. It was Hawkins who sifted through the hundreds of letters that landed in Ohio begging for an invitation, churning out one polite apology after another. Good wishes flooded in from friends, family, fans and film industry insiders; tellingly, the only person who wasn't in a hurry to wish the couple well was Howard Hawks. He remained pointedly silent.

Even without invitations, people began to turn up in Mansfield. Some brought tents, most brought cameras, but all came giddy with the hope that they might catch a glimpse of the happy couple. Crowds of pressmen and photographers clustered in town and around the farm and George Hawkins was expected to play ringmaster to the whole crazy circus. Despite the cool exterior that seemed to suggest that there was nothing he couldn't do, Hawkins assured friends that he wouldn't be in a rush to arrange another wedding anytime soon.

Bogie had been divorced for a week or so when he and Betty boarded the Santa Fe Super Chief in Pasadena, bound for Ohio. All of the stolen meetings and deceit, the disapproval and heartache, had led the couple to this idyllic corner of America, and the place where they would be wed. Hawkins collected them at the station and drove them to Malabar, where they would enjoy just two nights together before Bogie had to be back in Hollywood. When *Life* suggested that their photographer could travel along with the couple, Bogie retorted sharply 'maybe he'd like to photograph us fucking'. He had little time for the press.

The couple's blood tests were conducted on the evening of their arrival, whilst Bogie and Betty made a brief public appearance early on their wedding day when they visited the town courthouse to secure their licence. Photographers were clustered outside to snap Betty looking glam despite the fact that her freshly curled hair was concealed beneath a headscarf to keep it in place for the noon ceremony. Natalie came along too, as 20-year-old Betty needed parental consent to marry, and she was happy to give it.

Though Natalie would be matron of honour when her daughter tied the knot, it was only fitting that the Bromfield family would be central to the ceremony too. Louis Bromfield would serve as best man and his daughter, Hope, was poised to play the wedding march from Wagner's *Lohengrin*. In the absence of Betty's long-absent father, George Hawkins would give the bride away.

Once Betty and Bogie were back at Malabar, Betty told her fiancé that they couldn't risk bad luck, so they wouldn't be seeing each other again until the ceremony. For a girl who didn't believe in traditions, Betty sure was keen on them. Just as her nerves had left her trembling before a camera, now they reared again as she prepared to marry the man she adored. Meanwhile, an anxious Bogie paced the ground floor, sipping the latest in a string of nerve-steadying martinis.

On screen, Steve and Slim exuded easy confidence, but in that Ohio farmhouse, both were terrified. For Bogie, it was a last chance to finally find the settled homelife that had eluded him since childhood. His relationship with Mayo had left him shattered and, far from the self-possessed hard men he played on screen, the real Bogie was emotionally fragile. If this fourth marriage to a woman who was young enough to be his daughter didn't work out, things didn't look bright for the hard-drinking leading man. Betty, meanwhile, was racked with fear about the impending ceremony. She wanted it more than anything, but that didn't make her any less anxious.

By the time Betty completed the last of several bathroom pitstops and gathered up the white orchids that would serve as her bouquet, every bit of her was trembling. In his grey suit and with a gardenia in his buttonhole, Bogie was just as antsy, but at the centre of the proceedings was one attendee who was the very picture of calm. Prince, one of the Malabar boxer dogs, was parked on Judge Schettler's feet, enjoying the best seat in the house.

Bogie wept as he listened to the wedding vows and realised for the first time what they really meant. It had taken him four turns around the track, but on that day in May the importance of the promises he was making hit him in the heart. He couldn't have chosen a better place than Malabar Farm, a better friend than Louis Bromfield, nor a better organiser than George Hawkins.

Betty shook all the way through the brief ceremony, so much so that when Bogie tried to put her wedding ring on her finger, it stuck for a second before it slid easily into place. They had shared simmering love scenes in front of audiences worldwide, but when the time came for the bride and groom to kiss, a bashful Betty offered her husband her cheek. Weeping with emotion, Bogie took her in his arms and hugged her as he whispered, 'Hello, Baby.' And just like that, Bogie and Betty were one.

Betty turned and threw her bouquet to the guests; it was caught by Hope Bromfield. A moment later, the cake was brought in, champagne was poured and the cameras began snapping from every angle. The calm was replaced by organised chaos and at the heart of it were Bogie and Betty, radiant with happiness and looking forward to their shared future.

For a wedding gift, Bromfield gave the couple a boxer puppy named Harvey and an acre of land at Malabar, a place that they could always look on as their symbolic home in Ohio. Harvey became the youngest member of the Bogart–Bacall family, and he was a great peacemaker. He slept in the newlyweds' bedroom and, when they argued, went growling from one to the other until they had no choice but to reconcile just to settle his wounded nerves. The only place Harvey wasn't willing to follow his family was onto their boat. Devoted he might be, but a nautical hound he was not. Bogie had another answer to marital arguments too: 'We believe in double beds. It's pretty hard to sulk over something if you share the same bed.'

Though Betty gave Bogie the key to the couple's new home as a gift, they couldn't move in straight away. Instead, they settled into Bogie's old haunt at the Garden of Allah, where they found another mountain of telegrams waiting. The telephone was still ringing off the hook with good wishes and congratulations as the couple went back to work. It was to be Betty's first experience of the harsh reality of Hollywood. She had the extraordinary good fortune to make her debut in a hit. For the follow-up, she wouldn't be anything like so lucky.

Confidential Agent

Betty was in the make-up chair by dawn on the day after her return from Ohio, and on set soon after that. Bogie visited her to wish her well, but his good wishes weren't enough to carry her to another triumph. *Confidential Agent* was not a natural fit for the new wunderkind at Warners. She was cast, or rather miscast, as a British aristocrat opposite Charles Boyer in the adaptation of Graham Greene's novel of espionage and the Spanish Civil War. It was only her third film and the first without Bogie; it was also her first attempt at playing an Englishwoman, and from the off Betty struggled. Director Herman Shumlin was from the old school of film-making and on set, it was his way or no way. He offered little in the way of guidance or assistance despite Betty's pleas for help, instead leaving her to tussle with a role that she was woefully unprepared for.

Ironically, Betty had once spent a solid couple of weeks attempting to meet Shumlin when she was trying to make it in New York; now she finally had made it, the dream wasn't quite living up to the reality. Things weren't helped when Shumlin asked his leading lady to remove her wedding ring and the charm bracelet Bogie had bought her, a request she refused. Though it wasn't exactly war on set, nor was it a happy place. The realities of life as a working wife were coming home to roost too, and Betty was struggling to balance her schedule with her desire to take a trip with Bogie. With *Confidential Agent* still shooting and Bogie's own commitments looming large, it seemed impossible to find any time to spend together.

That was one of the reasons why the Bogarts' bungalow in the Garden of Allah and their subsequent home on Kings Road offered such a welcome respite. The Hollywood press was filled with gleeful reports that Bogie had lost his head for Betty, paying twice what the house was worth just because his wife fell in love with it at first sight. Yet in a town where newsprint could be savage, the Bogarts were welcomed with indulgent joy. As the presses rolled, Betty spent her free time preparing the honeymoon house on Kings Road ready for the move. She inherited Bogie's loyal domestic staff, who were more like members of the family, and who welcomed Betty to the household. It was one of those loyal staff who gave her the shock of a lifetime after hearing a radio announcer report – wrongly – that Betty was already expecting. When she and Bogie arrived home from a sailing trip the butler threw open the door and announced, 'I hear, my lady, we are blessed eventing. I do hope it's a boy.'

There was no pregnancy just yet, but there was a whole lot of romance. To show his appreciation of her efforts to build them a home, Bogie gave his new wife a mink coat. When Betty spread it on the floor and walked over it, relishing the feeling of the mink between her toes, he was overjoyed. There was a shameless decadence about her that some part of him envied. Betty was loving how grown up she felt too. Under her minor contract, her earnings had been placed in trust until she reached her twenty-first birthday, but as a married woman she successfully petitioned the courts for emancipation. Betty was legally ruled an adult in the summer of 1945. On top of that, newspapers were keen to assure readers that she had perfected the necessary skills to be not only a leading lady, but a wife too.

> LAUREN BACALL has added new accomplishments since she married Humphrey Bogart, and had sessions of romance with Charles Boyer in 'Confidential Agent.' She has learned to sail, to cook a simple meal, to hang drapes and to repair sails.[17]

Things were changing for Bogie as well. Sluggy the dog was renamed Slim and Sluggy the boat was sold, replaced by a 54-foot yawl called *Santana*, the name of the vessel Bogie would sail in *Key Largo* and the moniker he eventually gave his own production company. When Bogie's contract was renewed by Warners, he walked away with a fifteen-year commitment, a pair of golden handcuffs unprecedented in the history of the industry. Under the new deal negotiated by his agent, Sam Jaffe, Bogie was to make one movie per year for an eyewatering $200,000, subject to his approval of script and director. The contract also guaranteed him one picture per year away from Warners too. Endorsements and shrewd deals saw his average earnings skyrocket to $450,000, landing him the title of the highest-paid actor in Hollywood. As he left his handprints on the Walk of Fame in front of Grauman's Chinese Theater, surely even the ever-pessimistic Humphrey Bogart realised that he'd finally made it to the top.

Once the couple moved into their new home, life settled into a gentle routine. The fights that had plagued Bogie's marriage to Mayo were alien to Betty, whose nature was the polar opposite of her predecessor. The honeymoon period went on and on and on and the couple revelled not only in their intimacy, but in finally getting to know one another as only lovers can. But Bogie's sanctuary had always been a boat on the ocean and he was keen to share that passion with Betty as soon as their schedules allowed. With perfect timing, the couple left for their honeymoon in Catalina on the very day that a plumbing failure flooded their new home. Leaving the house to the contractors, they boarded Bogie's boat and sailed into the sunset.

Betty, so keen to love everything that her husband enjoyed, was determined to become a natural sailor too. Instead, the city gal was racked with sea sickness for the entire duration of the two-hour journey, taking little comfort in Bogie's assurances that she'd soon discover her sea legs. But for Betty Bogart, nausea was a small price to pay for the happy life that now lay before her.

One thing the Bogarts always agreed on was that Bogie wouldn't use his clout to push her career forward, though they both knew that the marriage came with implicit professional advantages for a blossoming starlet. Likewise, when it came to Betty continuing her career or potentially giving it up, Bogie wasn't about to say anything at all. 'I don't think she is the greatest actress in the business,' was his characteristically frank opinion of his wife. 'She has talents of a very high order, but I'm equally certain that she'd be a wonderful wife or mother.'[18] The choice was Betty's to make.

From the off, Betty knew that *Confidential Agent* was a bad move. Director Herman Shumlin lacked the guiding hand of either Hawks or Huston and without Bogie on set to offer advice, the experience was miserable. Shumlin had enjoyed a long career directing Broadway shows but *Confidential Agent* was only his second film, and his manner of handling actors would have set anyone's teeth on edge. He gave unwanted notes when things were going well, but offered no guidance when it was needed; when he wanted attention on set, he whistled with both fingers as though summoning a sheepdog, and Betty bristled. The unhappy shoot showed in the finished movie, which was castigated by critics.

> Miss Bacall, with more dialog than in her first pic, *To Have and Have Not* (her second unreleased as yet, is *The Big Sleep*, and *Agent* is her third), suffers from a monotony of voice and an uncertainty of performance. Her s.a. [sex appeal], however, is still plenty evident.[19]

The Bogarts were in Balboa when *Confidential Agent* opened. As the reviews came in, Betty's worst fears were realised and her confidence plummeted. The more unhappy she became, the more helpless Bogie felt. He needed to make it better, but he knew from bitter experience that it was something that came to all actors eventually; they just had to tough it

97

out. Betty, however, had been lauded so early and so highly that she felt every bruise of the critical drubbing. Eventually Bogie stopped commiserating and started kidding, teasing his wife until her tears turned to laughter.

Betty had another, perhaps more unexpected, champion. Novelist Graham Greene, never a fan of adaptations of his works, reserved a surprisingly special place in his heart for the movie that was made out of *Confidential Agent*. He was eventually moved to defend it – and Betty – against the critical brickbats.

> Mr Philip Purser writes that Lauren Bacall was 'insanely miscast in her third picture The Confidential Agent and having given – as she admits – a lousy performance, she nevertheless bitterly resented the cool notices that came her way'. I also as the author of the book resented those cool notices. This remains the only good film ever made from one of my books by an American director and Miss Bacall gave an admirable performance and so did Charles Boyer. For some reason the English critics thought a young American actress should not have played an English 'Honourable'. However the Honourable in my book was only removed by one generation from a coal miner and to me there seemed to be an extraordinary chauvinism and snobbism in their criticisms. Her performance was admirable.[20]

One has to sympathise with Betty. She was launched to a fanfare, trumpeted as the vamp to end all vamps and the most exciting female star to emerge in years, but she had no preparation for what being on that rarefied pedestal would be like. She was a sheltered unknown who had lived with her mother all her life, utterly dazzled by the glare of the Hollywood spotlight. Bogie and Betty were public property and just as quickly as an idol is raised, it can be torn down. Even as the reviews for *Confidential Agent* landed like bricks, the movie pressbook encouraged local cinemas to organise contests to find 'a lovely local Lauren Bacall', who would appear on the opening night of the movie and gamely smoulder at patrons with her own version of Betty's already notorious look. After all, what gal would turn down 'the opportunity that every woman desires – to be feted and admired'?

Betty had been feted and admired for *To Have and Have Not*, but the time had come for her to be dragged back down to earth. In an article entitled 'In Defense of My Wife', Bogie shared his thoughts on the reaction to *Confidential Agent*, though he had tussled with himself over whether or not to accept the assignment at all. He knew full well that Betty was more than capable of speaking for herself, but he knew too that her experience had left her reeling, and Bogie was an old-fashioned sort of gentleman at heart. Chivalry was hardwired into him.

> [Before] she had time to catch her breath, she took a panning that would have staggered even a seasoned star. The plain fact of the matter is that Betty was lauded for one picture out of all proportion to her desserts and panned for another that wasn't by any means her entire fault ... What I think is unfair is that Betty was the target for what the critics admitted was a poor picture. She didn't write it, she didn't direct it, she didn't play all the parts. Yet the critics acted as if the whole thing were her fault. They went out of their way to knock her just as they had to build her up.[21]

Yet for Betty, the unhappy experience of *Confidential Agent* came at a pivotal moment. She was content in her life with Bogie and had been thinking a lot about the future even before her critical mauling. As far as she could see, there were two options available: she could put her career first, or abandon it for a life as a wife and, she hoped, mother. Bogie had already lost two wives to their careers but he didn't try to sway Betty's decision; it was important that she make the choice for herself. Betty flipflopped back and forth, on one day ready to give it all up and on the next determined to show her critics that she wasn't a one-hit wonder. She knew that Bogie thought that she'd been treated unfairly, and he knew that the decision had to be hers.

Bogie showed an understandable sensitivity in his reading of the situation. Betty was riding high as a *Harper's Bazaar* cover girl when she was plucked from obscurity and groomed for stardom by would-be Svengali Howard Hawks. When she fell for Bogie, Hawks's nose wasn't put out of joint so much as knocked clean off his face. He couldn't bully her, manipulation failed and cajoling didn't work, so he dropped his protégé like a stone and sold her contract to Warners. *The Big Sleep* was the last film Betty and Hawks made together. On top of that, she was caught in the blast from Mayo and Bogie's emotional shrapnel right at the moment of her Hollywood launch. Of course, Betty didn't have to stay in the middle of that, but love can do funny things to a 19-year-old. Who among us didn't think they were about as mature as it gets at that age, and who among us can honestly say that they didn't believe, hand on heart, that they knew best?

Then came the press tour, the reunion with family and friends, the divorce and engagement and the wedding heard all over the world. Betty was flying higher than ever, and *Confidential Agent* brought her back down to earth with a bone-shaking bump. It was the mid-1940s, a time when married women were still traditionally homemakers, just as Mayo had tried to become. Betty had dreams of being a perfect wife too, with a frilly pinny and a meal on the table. She even pictured herself in a farmhouse just like Malabar, where she would carry pails of freshly drawn milk into a cosy kitchen for the husband who waited with a welcome-home kiss.

Benedict Canyon

The Bogarts started on the path to what would be a short-lived dream of their own rural idyll when they left Kings Road to move to 2707 Benedict Canyon Road. Bogie was doubtful about the move to the countryside from the off and it soon appeared as though his doubts were well-placed. Beset by trouble from flash floods and rattlesnakes, city-kid Betty quickly realised that it wasn't the place for her. For a kid from Manhattan, there was such a thing as too much peace and quiet. Besides, she had difficult decisions to make and work and home lay at the heart of them.

'If my career interferes with our domestic life, it's best that I give it up,' she said in 1946, just before *Confidential Agent* came out and dropped a depth charge on her career.

> Bogie loves a home. He likes to come home to his meals, stay home and share it with his friends. I feel that a wife should be in a home. She should be there to see that it is run properly – not leave it in the hands of strangers. When I have children I want to raise them myself – not force them to get used to a strange nurse who takes the place of their mother.[22]

She had already seen her fair share of Hollywood divas who enjoyed 'Big mansions and empty hearts'.[23] Though there were certainly Hollywood leading ladies who had both families and careers, Betty felt as though she had to make a decision to be one or the other, but her mind was changing with every moment that passed.

For some people, the critical reception that greeted *Confidential Agent* would've been enough to make the decision for them. Few would've blamed Betty if she'd retreated to Benedict Canyon to lick her wounds, but that would've been underestimating Betty Bacall. Don't forget that this was the girl who'd trekked the streets of New York flogging copies of

Actor's Cue, knocking on the door of every producer and grafting all day long with the intention of reaching the brass ring. *To Have and Have Not* had put in just within her grasp, and she was damned if *Confidential Agent* was going to snatch it away. Baby might be her nickname, but it certainly wasn't her personality.

> THE spanking 'Baby' Bacall took from the critics for her performance in 'Confidential Agent' has worked in a strange fashion. It caught her in the midst of trying to decide between an acting career and settling down as just not-so-plain Mrs. Humphrey Bogart. Now her fighting spirit is up. She's determined to get in there and show everyone that what happened to her in 'Confidential Agent' wasn't her fault – and shouldn't happen to 'The Look.' Wrong casting and continued clashing with the director seem to head the list of reasons.[24]

Betty showed plenty of Bogart-esque guts when she owned up to the fact that she hadn't exactly set the screen on fire in *Confidential Agent*. She knew it from the start, but neither the studio nor Shumlin would release her from the movie. When the film came out, Betty shouldered the blame for its failure precisely because she was the new kid on the lot. Charles Boyer was a tried and tested star with a list of critical successes to his name and Shumlin's Broadway record spoke for itself. With just one film on her CV and *The Big Sleep* in the can, it was inevitably Betty who took the mauling. The girl known to some as the Million Dollar Bubble had seen her bubble burst.

As if that wasn't enough, word reached Bogie that the Hollywood Women's Press Club was looking to award Betty the far from coveted title of Most Uncooperative Actress of the Year. Her only competition was Greer Garson, whose career could brush off such a supposedly playful insult, but Betty was stunned. She couldn't understand what she'd done to deserve it, especially since she'd followed the studio's three-line whip on press. Luckily Bogie had a plan to take the sting off. He called every journalist he knew and told them to vote for Betty, turning the insult into the punchline to an affectionate joke. In the event, despite Bogie's best efforts, the dubious honour went to Mrs Miniver instead.

Yet Betty wasn't the sort of woman who ran away from a challenge, no matter how badly bruised she was. Betty wasn't about to be counted out. She was determined to come back swinging and show the world that there was a lot more to her than a marriage certificate and The Look.

But what of Bogie, the hard-drinking triple-divorcee who had finally got his fairy-tale ending? He didn't pour the contents of his whisky bottles down the drain and nor did Betty ask him to. Instead, she was there at his side when he needed her, offering the sort of emotional security that he had never known in his life and never dared to ask for. The very thing that seemed to have doomed their relationship from the off, namely Betty's youth, was precisely what made it work. She brought no baggage into the marriage, only optimism and self-belief, and that made her the ideal candidate to help Bogie shoulder his own considerable burden. He was a pessimist, she an optimist, and she could see it in what she called his 'cocker spaniel eyes'. 'Even when he's happiest, Bogie's eyes are sad,' Betty observed, and she knew her husband better than anyone. 'It worried me. Now I know.'[25]

What she knew was that Bogie had learned to expect the worst, no matter how well things were going, but she had underestimated how hardened life had left him. An incident early in their marriage brought home to Betty that her husband was far from a white knight, and gave her a dose of unvarnished truth. Tragically, Betty's beloved cocker spaniels, Droopy and Puddle, were hit by a car, killing Droopy and leaving Puddle injured, though she would recover. Betty was alone when she received the news, whilst Bogie was out boozing. When he finally called home to ask how her night was going, he was loaded.

Betty spilled her heart out to Bogie, who invited her to join him and his buddy for a consoling drink. She arrived to find the men drunk as skunks and in no mood to sympathise; humiliated, angry and grieving, Betty left them to it. The Bogarts didn't see each other again until breakfast, when Bogie staggered over the threshold of their home and passed out. When he came to, he was ashamed; the incident marked the start of a change in Humphrey Bogart. Eaten up by guilt for letting his grieving wife down when she needed him most, Bogie swore to do better. To his credit, he just about managed it. He still drank, but not as much, and when he did go on a bender, Betty didn't shout or rail against it. Instead, she did the precise opposite: she ignored him. That was the only tactic that seemed to work on Bogie, and the more Betty ignored him, the better Bogie behaved.

The one thing that he couldn't govern so easily was his addiction to nicotine. It's rare to see a leading man smoke on film today, but back then, it was rare not to. And nobody smoked more than Humphrey Bogart. When one thinks of what made Bogie Bogie, there are some props that seem inseparable from the man: namely, the trench coat, fedora and cigarette. Lucrative endorsement deals from Chesterfield – he smoked two packs a day – all went towards making him the highest-paid actor in Hollywood, but he certainly enjoyed the products he was paid to advertise in his personal life too.

Much speculation has existed over Bogie's relationships with other women during his marriage to Betty, but those who knew the couple claim there weren't any. Bogie wasn't interested in playing around when he was married to Betty, and had no appetite for the chase in middle age. On the occasions when a woman did get too close, Betty stepped in and saw her off with a cool word. As she reflected once, 'invisible chains last longer', and unlike Mayo, she never resorted to violence. Instead, she spoiled Bogie rotten, especially when it came to his Christmas birthday. No longer would he feel cheated out of a celebration, because Betty threw everything she had into making the day one to remember, no matter how many Christmases the couple spent together. In fact, those Christmases would be painfully few in number.

Mr and Mrs Bogart

Though Betty was determined to rebuild her career after the debacle of *Confidential Agent*, it was no easy task. *The Big Sleep* had sat on the shelf as the studio rushed out its remaining slew of war pictures, wanting to get them into cinemas before the public's appetite for victory began to ebb and Betty began to fear she'd be forgotten. After Betty's unhappy experience with *Confidential Agent*, Charles Feldman petitioned the studio to film new scenes that would capitalise on the enduring public interest in Betty and Bogie's romance, and up the sizzle quotient considerably. It was a masterstroke; of course Hawks knew exactly what tone was required for the inserts.

> It was during the racing season at Santa Anita and I had some horses out there, so I made them talk about riding a horse and it ended with that line, 'It depends on who's in the saddle.' Well, that was just me thinking about racing, so I thought I'd do a little love argument about racing. [The plot] didn't matter at all. All we were trying to do was to make every scene entertain. I can't follow the story.[26]

Despite the best efforts of Hawks and uncredited screenwriter Julius Epstein, it still didn't seem to be enough. With the other actresses on the cast threatening to eclipse the leading lady, unforgiving cuts had to be made to turn Betty into the star of the show. *The Big Sleep*'s author, Raymond Chandler, recalled that Martha Vickers outperformed Betty in every scene they shared; as a result, most of her scenes were cut to keep the focus on the woman at the top.

After *Confidential Agent*, Betty pinned her hopes on *The Big Sleep*, but she was to be dealt another disappointment. The recut and reshot film rendered an already complicated plot even more baffling, but even a distinct sense of disjointed confusion couldn't kill this now-classic noir.

Bogie garnered plenty of plaudits for his performance and Vickers and Dorothy Malone were singled out for praise, but for Betty the raves were few and far between. In the *New York Times*, Bosley Crowther summed up the worst of them when he remarked that 'Miss Bacall is a dangerous looking female, but she still hasn't learned to act.'[27] The problem was, she'd simply been outgunned. Despite that, she wasn't lambasted as she had been on *Confidential Agent*. Rather, the critics decided that whilst Betty might not be quite as deserving of their plaudits as she had been in *To Have and Have Not*, she was certainly better as a vamp opposite Bogie than as an English aristo opposite Charles Boyer. It was enough to stave off total despair, but Betty later lamented that she had never been able to recapture the magic of *To Have and Have Not*, no matter how hard she tried.

At home, Bogie and Betty had all they wanted, and perhaps that was why she didn't feel the failure as deeply as she might have otherwise. But Betty's childhood dreams hadn't been of marriage, they'd been of stardom. With precious little formal training in how to act, let alone how to handle the sort of white-hot media and public interest that accompanied her debut, it's no wonder that she foundered when her subsequent projects didn't prove her earlier promise. Years later, Betty admitted to a perfectly understandable occasional bitterness that she was thought of as Mrs Bogart first and an actress second, but there's no doubt that Mrs Bogart loved that particular role above any other. It wasn't only Bogie who needed someone to come home to.

Yet it wasn't all wine and roses. Bogie and Betty were at different stages of life and though their marriage was certainly a very happy one, it wasn't without its differences. Bogie had lived in splendour as a child before he was reduced to playing chess for pennies on the street, but even when he reached the heights of Hollywood, he had no interest in returning to the luxury that had once cushioned the famed Humphrey Baby. His loyal and long-serving domestic staff brought an air of eccentricity rather than formality to the home and standing on ceremony was the last thing on anybody's mind. Though Bogie's lifestyle was increasingly modest, he had met his polar opposite in Betty.

Betty, the girl who had always wondered what it would be like to walk on mink, now knew the answer. And she loved it. She had never known the luxury of her husband's childhood, but once she was one half of the most famous duo in Hollywood, she started to spend. The couple's home filled up with shoes and designer dresses, expensive keepsakes and antiques by the dozen. Bogie was happy to indulge his Baby with heartfelt gifts of his own, including a gold cigarette case that was fastened with a ruby clasp and bore the inscription, 'For Mrs Me who never need whistle for Bogie.'

The man who had once drunk the town dry now preferred evenings at home, whilst Betty wanted to sample everything that stardom could offer. 'He says I was great, did everything he wanted until I got him in my clutches,'[28] she joked, but her influence on Bogie was anything but the fruit of manipulation; she offered stability and just enough indulgence. She didn't impose rules on when Bogie drank, how much or who with, and soon learned that hosting his drinking pals was preferable to him going out boozing. Bogie's home was his sanctuary, subconsciously or otherwise, and he wanted it to remain that way.

Sadly for Bogie, his greatest passion was one that his wife never quite shared. Though Betty had done her best to learn to sail, she accepted that 'yachting is something you must have in your blood, and I definitely don't'.[29] It was definitely in Bogie's blood, so when he disappeared into the Pacific for days on end, Betty let him go. Spending time alone rejuvenated Bogie just as spending time with friends rejuvenated Betty. They were always happier together, but time apart kept the fires burning.

The power dynamic in Bogie and Betty's relationship, for there certainly was one, might have surprised those who worried for the sheltered young girl marrying the grizzled man of the world. Betty had been raised by a strong-willed and independent single mother, who wouldn't take any nonsense from anyone. The trembling wannabe matured into a marriage that had made her one of the queens of Hollywood and as she did, the inner Natalie began to emerge. Betty had a seam of toughness running through her bones and when she needed it, a whipcrack of a tongue. Mayo's drunken aggression was out of control, but Betty wasn't subject to the same alcoholic chaos: hers was a no-nonsense approach. Two violent drunks led to smashed crockery and mocking headlines, but a drunk and a woman who could keep him in line was a much more manageable state of affairs. They found a happy middle ground on socialising and travel, something Betty loved but Bogie avoided, and when Betty set her mind on something, she generally got it. One of the few things on which Bogie was immovable was his loathing of people dropping by unannounced at the house, which the extended Bacall family was wont to do. But if that was the only sticking point, it was a long way from guns and knives.

Though Bogie always maintained that he wouldn't pull strings for Betty, when he thought a film might be right for her, he spoke up. So it was with *Dead Reckoning*, which Bogie was making on loan for Columbia. Bogie didn't want to go, since Warners could cream off and keep any extra money over and above his salary, but since he was stuck with it, he was determined to get Betty on board. The movie had initially been intended as a vehicle for Rita Hayworth and Bogie, but with Hayworth refusing to work during a contract dispute, Bogie mentioned Betty's name. Jack Warner refused point blank to loan her out and the role went instead to Lizabeth Scott, who was being promoted as 'The Threat', in a not-so-subtle riff on Betty's nickname, 'The Look'. Like Betty, Scott was a sultry former model with a line in vampish smouldering, but this time the finished product fell far short of recreating the magic of *To Have and Have Not*.

Dark Passage

In 1947, the Bogarts teamed up again to make *Dark Passage* with director Delmer Davies. The film is particularly notable for its first hour or so, which is told from the subjective point of view of Bogie's character as he recovers from extensive plastic surgery. Only once his bandages are removed to reveal Bogart beneath do we see him for the first time. Though it's an unusual technique, it wasn't the first movie to try it. Just a year earlier, Robert Montgomery had succeeded in realising his passion project, *Lady in the Lake*, which is shot almost entirely from the lead's point of view. In *Lady in the Lake*, the technique is anything but an unqualified success, but *Dark Passage* pulled it off with panache. It also had the sense to use the first-person point of view within limits, rather than without compromise, and employed traditional filmmaking techniques once the plot approached its denouement.

Shot on location in San Francisco, *Dark Passage* tells the story of Vincent Parry, unjustly imprisoned in San Quentin after being wrongly convicted of murdering his wife. When Parry escapes, he takes shelter with Betty's Irene Jansen and submits to surgery in order to conceal his identity so that he can solve the murder and clear his name. Of course, Irene is soon dragged in on the way to the inevitable happy ending – though wrongs are far from righted as the lights go up.

The true star of *Dark Passage* is undoubtedly the dramatic San Francisco landscape, laced with shadows and rich with hints of danger. It's a city made for film noir and *Dark Passage* doesn't disappoint. Freed from the confines of the studio lot the camera can take in the full sweep of San Francisco, capturing not only the stark dangers facing our heroes, but the heart of the city that could offer shelter or turn against them.

Dark Passage gave Betty something more to do than embody Howard Hawks's ideal woman. Her character is introduced not as the sultry, vampish sexpot on which she had made her name, but as the sort of down-to-earth gal who crops up all too rarely in film noir. By the time the inner vamp reveals herself, Betty had already shown audiences that she could flex a few different character muscles.

Though the challenges of *Dark Passage* for Betty were professional, for Bogie they were more personal. During the final stages of the shoot, once the couple had left their temporary home at Mark Hopkins Hotel in San Francisco for the Hollywood backlot, Bogie's anxiety had reached a peak. A lifetime of drink and stress led to a vitamin deficiency that resulted in alopecia areata and his hair began to fall out at a worrying rate. Though the actor had worn a hairpiece for years, by the time *Dark Passage* wrapped, he was reluctantly wearing a full wig on camera. Bogie had never been a vain man, but the loss of his hair hit him so hard that he swallowed his pride and consulted a doctor. With treatment and the proper nutrition, the condition could be reversed, but he was increasingly having to accept that his hard-living lifestyle was coming back to haunt him as he grew older.

The Bogart–Bacall marriage was one that enjoyed a very particular dynamic, and perhaps not quite the dynamic that anyone had been expecting. At the start it had seemed like a well-worn story, as an older man with a string of failed and volatile relationships behind him fell for the beguiled and beguiling younger woman. Or perhaps it was more cynical than even that, as a girl with ambition caught herself an established star who would make her name even if the movies didn't. But there was much more to it. Betty loved the good life that Bogie had often eschewed. She wanted to travel and surround herself with nice things and she had the tenacity and stubborn streak to get her way. Bogie shared that same stubborn streak and somehow, it just worked. Betty was determined to get what she wanted but what she wanted most of all was a healthy, happy husband. The Battling Bogarts were in the past.

Though it seemed as if the couple had it all, that wasn't quite the truth. Betty's movie debut had established her as the sort of instant megastar that comes along once in a blue moon, but the follow-ups had been lacklustre. Without Howard Hawks behind the camera, she failed to live up to her earlier promise. Nobody was more aware of that than Betty, who desperately wanted to prove herself with different kinds of project. When Jack Warner ignored her complaints about the roles on offer, she followed her husband's lead and started turning them down. The more she said no, the more insistent Warner became until Betty was placed on suspension.

Once again, Betty's thoughts turned to matters domestic. She had always wanted a family and she envisioned the house in Benedict Canyon as the perfect place to raise her children. Bogie had reservations about the move and now he had reservations about parenthood too. After three failed marriages, he was worried that a baby would rock the happy boat, selfish though that may seem. As the couple started work on *Key Largo*, he had something else he had always wanted too, a wife who was there at his side at home and away, rather than pursuing a career on the far side of the continent. Essentially, now Bogie had found the love of his life, he feared losing her to their child. Yet Betty was young and desperate to become a mother. Mindful that not starting a family with his wife might prove to be the thing that ended up costing him his marriage, Bogie agreed.

Key Largo

For three years, the couple tried without success to conceive. When medical tests revealed that Bogie's sperm count was low, he agreed to a series of hormone shots that kickstarted more anxiety and hair loss. Heartened by her husband's observation that sex was the most fun a couple could have without laughing, Betty kept one eye on her calendar and the other on the bedroom. In the spring of 1948, she finally received the news she had been praying for: she was pregnant. To her dismay, Bogie was anything but delighted. Instead of celebrating, he flew into a rage, telling Betty that he wasn't going to let any baby steal her away; it was the biggest fight the couple had ever had, and what should have been a moment of joy was one of bitter recriminations instead. Back in the old days, Bogie would've chased it up with a drinking binge and disappeared for a week or two, but the old days were gone. When the next morning came, a repentant Bogie presented Betty with a heartfelt letter of apology,

108

admitting that what lay behind his outburst wasn't anger, but fear. He was to become a father at nearly 50 years old and the thought terrified him. Peace was restored: they'd go through it together, for better or worse.

Yet Bogie was still Bogie and as Betty celebrated with a baby shower, the expectant father raised hell at a stag party instead. As the booze flowed, he drunkenly acted out the part of a woman in labour, whose baby would be delivered by a hearth-tong wielding John Huston. Things only got more raucous when Betty and her friends threw on men's suits and crashed the party. Bogie wasn't entirely reformed, but as the evening tumbled into sentimental chaos, nor was he the hellraiser he used to be either.

As Betty's pregnancy progressed, Bogie was working on his career. *The Treasure of the Sierra Madre*, which teamed him with Huston again in a tale of luckless treasure seekers in Mexico, opened to rave reviews. Betty had joined Bogie on the difficult location shoot and had watched her husband give one of the finest performances of his career. As the paranoid Fred C. Dobbs, he and friends played by Tim Holt and Walter Huston find themselves increasingly at odds as they search for the titular treasure. Together, they created another legend.

The all-male cast clashed with each other and director Huston, and it was only Betty's intervention that kept him from flattening Bogie during a particularly heated confrontation. *The Treasure of the Sierra Madre* was hailed as an instant classic; Jack Warner called it 'the greatest motion picture we have ever made', but it wrung Bogie out.

Though *Key Largo*'s reviews weren't as universally adoring, it gave Bogie another Huston-helmed hit. *Key Largo* reunited Bogie and Betty in a noir adaptation of Maxwell Anderson's play that was intended to show-case their strengths. The movie tells the story of Bogie's Frank McCloud, who visits the Hotel Largo to meet James Temple. Temple is the father of Frank's late army buddy, George, who was killed in the Italian campaign. A hurricane threatens to batter the Florida Keys and the hotel that serves a ragtag clientele. Frank gets to know the locals, including George's widow, Nora, played by Betty. The storm hits as a gang of desperate gangsters led by Edward G. Robinson's Johnny Rocco take James, Nora and Frank hostage, and a tense tale of double cross, violence, and heroism unfolds.

Thanks to the public's hunger for more Bacall–Bogart pairings and the always-popular presence of Edward G. Robinson, *Key Largo* outperformed *The Treasure of Sierra Madre* at the box office, arguably undeservedly. Though it's enormously entertaining, *Key Largo* could have given Betty something more to do: she's just too supplicant to Bogie, wide-eyed and adoring rather than teasing and sparring. Still, even adoring Betty and Bogie is better than none at all.

Key Largo was to be the last film in which Robinson and Bogart shared the screen and this time, top billing went to Bogart. But as a 1948 letter to *Time* magazine proved, he didn't let it go to his head.

> It has come to my attention that in your Current & Choice section, Lauren Bacall has consistently been left out of the cast of Key Largo.
>
> Inasmuch as there are those of us in Hollywood, Miss Bacall among them, who would rather make Current & Choice than win an Academy Award or make Men of Distinction, won't you please include her in the cast of Key Largo in Current & Choice just once, as she is my wife and I have to live with her. Miss Bacall is extremely tired of being labelled et al.[30]

Betty's name was added to *Current & Choice* in that same issue.

Bogart's first foray into film production came as the result of a personal tragedy. His friend, Mark Hellinger, had purchased the rights to Willard Motley's novel *Knock on Any Door*, and intended to cast Bogie as crusading lawyer Andrew Morton opposite Marlon Brando as Nick Romano, a kid from the slums facing death row for murder. Instead, when Hellinger died in 1947, Bogart established his own company, Santana Productions, to take the film forward. Though Brando was replaced by John Derek, Bogie stayed on and Nicholas Ray was chosen to direct.

After so many years struggling to make his voice heard, Bogie initially revelled in calling the business shots. He little suspected that Santana, which released most of its pictures through Columbia, would eventually cause more stress than joy. But as *Knock on Any Door* went into production, Betty was blooming.

Stephen

Betty's contractions began early on 6 January 1949. Buoyed by youthful confidence and having enjoyed a textbook pregnancy so far, Betty saw Bogie off to work on *Knock on Any Door*, then began timing her pains. When she eventually telephoned her trusted doctor, Red Krohn, he advised her to wait until the contractions were coming at five-minute intervals, then call again. As Betty watched the clock, she received an odd telephone call from Sheila Graham, the British gossip columnist behind the widely syndicated 'Hollywood Today' column, who wanted to know whether it was true that Bogie had fathered a child with another woman. Betty simply told her 'no', then ventured out to Krohn's office, where he arranged her admission to hospital and contacted Bogie, who rushed to meet his wife.

During their journey to the hospital, Betty told Bogie about Graham's telephone call. Channelling his anger into that seemed to take his mind off worrying about Betty, but by the time they reached the hospital, the Bogarts were entirely focused on their imminent new arrival. Bogie was determined to stay with his Baby and joined her in the delivery room, where the great screen hard man grew increasingly green about the gills. It wasn't the labour that was upsetting him, he explained, but the pain that the woman he loved was having to endure. Bogie eventually opted to wait outside as Betty delivered Stephen Humphrey Bogart just after 11.00 pm. Bogie greeted his wife and child with a teary, 'Hello, Baby,' as he was shown back into the room.

Whilst Betty and Stephen slumbered, Bogie headed off to Chasen's to hand out cigars and toast the newest Bogart on the scene, but at dawn he was back at Betty's bedside once more, miraculously still sober. When Los Angeles experienced its first snowfall in half a century during her hospital stay, Betty took it as the very best sort of omen for a couple of native New Yorkers. The snow was still thick on the ground when the little family arrived home two days later to be greeted by an enormous snowman that Bogie had built for his son. Any fears that Betty might have had about her husband's ability to adjust to the baby were quashed entirely when she heard the new father on the intercom they had rigged up in the nursery. The man who had grown famous for his portrayals of hard-bitten gangsters and no-nonsense heroes was gently welcoming his newborn child into the world. 'Hello, son,' Bogie whispered in a voice tender with wonder. 'You're a little fella, aren't you? I'm Father. Welcome home.'

Motherhood fulfilled Betty in a way that her struggling career had not. She had wanted to act more than anything but, when that dream came true, her smash-hit debut had proved to be a curse as much as a blessing. She had not been able to sustain the launch velocity that *To Have and Have Not* had provided and, given the roles that Warner forced on her, it's hardly a surprise. Yet despite Bogie's doubts about fatherhood – indeed, he remained a somewhat hands-off father in Steve's infancy – Betty was smitten by her new role. Much of Bogie's reticence was a result of his nagging fears, sadly realised, that he wouldn't live to see his children reach adulthood.

Whilst Betty threw herself into motherhood, little Steve was already making influential friends. The Bogarts had met Harry S. Truman during his successful campaign for the White House and Bogie and Truman placed a wager on whether he would be welcoming a son or a daughter. Truman won the bet and Bogie gallantly dispatched a cheque for twenty dollars to Pennsylvania Avenue. The cheque was returned uncashed, along with a letter from the new Commander-in-Chief. 'It is a rare instance when I find a man who remembers his commitments and meets them on the dot,' said Truman happily.

During Steve's first months, Bogie's professional life wasn't proving anything like as fulfilling as Betty's domestic set-up. *Knock on Any Door* didn't set the critics alight nor bring a fortune into Santana's coffers, and it gave Bogie a stark taste of the business of moviemaking. He followed it up with *Tokyo Joe*, in which Bogie starred as a war veteran tussling with Japanese gang bosses for the lives of the wife and child he abandoned. Eventually he makes the ultimate sacrifice, giving up the woman he loves so she can make her escape with the man who has taken his place. The propaganda elements of the film have aged like milk and though transplanted to the gambling dens of Tokyo, critics sniffed out that it was an unnecessary retread of *Casablanca*. For the public, however, the film's timely focus on post-war Japan proved fascinating enough to get them lining up at the ticket booth.

Bogie had set up Santana to escape the Hollywood treadmill and give himself the sort of roles that Warner Bros didn't offer. Ironically, *Tokyo Joe* found the leading man in exactly the type of part that he could've played with his eyes shut. He was savvy enough to realise that the public wanted to see Humphrey Bogart in a Humphrey Bogart role, but he wasn't getting the fulfilment he had hoped for. Instead, he was working twice as hard and wasn't reaping any of the rewards, whether they be artistic, personal or financial, that he had anticipated. Bogie had backed himself into a corner.

A Panda Party

It had been a long time since Bogie, reformed and in love as he now was, had been in the papers for his drunken escapades. That changed during a press junket to New York to publicise the release of *Tokyo Joe*, when he left an exhausted Betty at their hotel and went out boozing with friends. Drunk and stupid, the men acquired two large stuffed pandas and took them along for a party at El Morocco, a notorious celebrity drinking den on East 52nd Street.

In the early hours of that autumn morning, a wannabe model named Robin Roberts decided that she wanted a souvenir of the evening she'd spent in the same bar as Humphrey Bogart. She made a grab for one of the pandas but had reckoned without Bogie, who grabbed the bear and yanked it towards him. Robin hit the floor and her friend, Peggy Rabe, came running only to skid off her heels and land on her rump. Seeing their girlfriends in a heap, the gals' dates waded in and soon crockery and glasses were flying. It was just like the old days. 'It pointed up the hazards an actor can be subjected to while quietly sipping an early morning drink with a panda,'[31] noted the press wryly.

Starved of tales of Bogie's wild living for too long, the press went to town. By the time he appeared in court six days later, he had been splashed across the front pages alongside photos of Roberts, every inch the sultry girl in trouble. True to form, Bogie was in a scrupulously honest and pugilistic mood. He admitted to being drunk but vehemently denied that any violence had taken place. Arguing that 'I'm too sweet and chivalrous', he smelled a rat. Perhaps surprisingly given his reputation for booze and flying fists, the judge agreed.

The case was dismissed as one not of drunk and disorderly behaviour, but attempted extortion. Roberts and Rabe were chastised for fabricating a charge just to make money out of the actor, and were summarily dismissed from the courtroom. The owners of El Morocco took a different view. Regardless of blame, Bogie's boozy exploits had cost them money and bad publicity, and they barred him. Hot on their heels came a laundry list of other New York drinking joints who warned that Bogie and any other hard drinkers looking for trouble were on borrowed time. Any more bad behaviour and he wouldn't only be barred from one den, but dozens.

The incident gave Jack Warner just the excuse he'd been looking for to turn the screws on his star. Bogie's relationship with the mogul had never been happy and his efforts for Santana had not exactly set the box office alight, so Warner decided that the time was right for payback. It came in the shape of a pair of uninspiring movies that seemed almost deliberately designed to frustrate their star. *Chain Lightning* and *The Enforcer* were efficient pictures and nothing more, and Bogie felt himself sliding further into the very dissatisfaction that Santana had been intended to stave off. In fact, it was Betty and another *Santana* that provided the perfect remedy, and Bogie basked in the open horizon of the Pacific Ocean, turning his back on Hollywood in the most literal sense.

Betty had settled into her role of a devoted mother and was happy for her life to revolve around Steve. In keeping with her Hollywood lifestyle, Betty was aided by nurse Alice Hartley, but whenever Alice took a night off, Betty slept in the nursery to keep an eye on the sleeping Steve. Bogie wasn't too fond of that arrangement, which reignited his worries that he'd lose his wife to their son, but Betty was keen to provide concrete evidence that wasn't the case. To keep her husband happy, she made an effort to enjoy their breaks on board the *Santana*, despite being no fan of the ocean.

Alice Hartley's addition to the household wasn't only necessary so Betty and Bogie could take their secluded cruises, but because Betty was beginning to feel a little restless. She wanted to be a wife and mother, but she wanted to make movies too. If she was going to do both, she needed help, because Bogie certainly wasn't about to become a stay-at-home dad. Alice provided the perfect solution.

The Comeback

Betty's screen comeback was in *Young Man with a Horn*, a musical drama inspired by the life of Bix Beiderbecke. The picture saw Betty as Amy North, a troubled young woman whose affair with musician Rick Martin, played by Kirk Douglas, almost leads to his self-destruction. The role of the good girl was taken by Doris Day, who later recalled that her experience on the film had been made miserable by her leading man's cool persona. The film was to be directed by Michael Curtiz, the man behind *Casablanca*, and Betty couldn't wait to get to it. Though Day's experience on the set was an unhappy one, Betty was thrilled to be reunited with her old friend Douglas and if the resultant movie proved disappointing, her experience was anything but.

Betty was reunited with Curtiz on her follow-up, *Bright Leaf*, a drama starring Gary Cooper as a struggling inventor who hits the big time with a new method for manufacturing cigarettes. He uses his newfound fortune to avenge himself on the ruthless tobacco magnate who drove his father out of business, only to find himself double-crossed when he marries the magnate's vengeful daughter, played by Patricia Neal. It's an old-school morality tale loosely based on a true story and adapted from a novel by Foster Fitz-Simmons, in which money predictably buys our hero everything but happiness. It was no *Casablanca*.

114

In *Bright Leaf*, Betty plays Cooper's first love, Sonia, who has since grown up and prospered as the owner-operator of a brothel. She is the quintessential tart with a heart, whose unrequited love offers Cooper's Brant Royle his only chance of happiness. Naturally he throws it over for Neal's scheming Margaret Singleton, the woman who ruins him. By the time Brant realises what he has lost, it is too late; Sonia tells him that the man she loved is dead, replaced by one who has sacrificed his humanity for money, ambition and revenge.

In case you couldn't tell, it's a melodrama. Though critics praised the performances, the twists and turns of the plot surprised and charmed precisely nobody, leaving Betty to nurse yet another unfortunate blemish on her CV. She had been excited to start making movies again, but life had thrown a bucket of cold water over her enthusiasm.

Alice Hartley's arrival in the Bogart household didn't only allow Betty to get back to work, it also freed her to give Bogie the attention that he craved. She was mothering not only her son, but her husband. There were times when Bogie would tease her by explaining that he'd like a pocket-sized wife, who he could put away whenever he craved his own company; in fact, this favourite topic of his had even made it into *Dead Reckoning*'s screenplay. Yet in many ways, whenever Bogie headed out on the *Santana* or Betty ventured into the nursery to play with Steve, they had both achieved exactly that – a marriage that worked together but definitely benefited from a little time spent apart.

Throughout his career, Bogie had never been afraid of studio suspension and that attitude rubbed off on Betty. Frustrated by the scripts being presented to her, she started turning them down, only to find that she hated being idle more than she hated making sub-par movies. Much as she loved being Mrs Bogart, this ongoing artistic frustration convinced Betty that she didn't want to give up her career.

Bogie, meanwhile, had problems of his own. The quintessential image of a trench coat-wearing, cigarette-smoking and granite-faced hero had made a lot of money, but it had also become a source of parody and Bogie was tiring of being the butt of the joke. Santana had promised the opportunity to break away from those tired roles but instead it had only brought more of them, as the star found himself producing films in which he played up to his own typecasting. It was the only sure-fire way to bring audiences in. He returned to the familiar plot of *Casablanca* again with *Sirocco*, but the longing of Bogie and Bergman was nowhere to be seen between Hump and Marta Torén. Bogie's co-star was being marketed as the new Bergman now that Ingrid's affair with Roberto Rossellini had hit the headlines, but there was simply no sizzle in the script or on the screen. In the wake of *Sirocco*, Bogie badly needed a challenge; *Bold Venture*, a radio project he signed onto alongside Betty, definitely wasn't it.

Bold Venture saw Bogie star as the improbably named Slate Shannon, a hard-bitten sailor who runs his own hotel, Shannon's Place, in Cuba. There he is joined by his sultry ward, Sailor Duval, and a ragtag group of revolutionaries, treasure seekers and pirates, all of whom have a story to tell. Sailing the seas aboard their boat, the *Bold Venture* of the title, Sailor and Slate adventure around the Caribbean saving the day and flirting up a storm.

Bold Venture was a hark back to the Bogie and Betty of *To Have and Have Not*, and Shannon's Place even had a resident musician in the mould of *Casablanca*'s Sam to keep the plot bouncing along. The show was syndicated through the USA and made its stars $10,000 a week, but it was no *To Have and Have Not*. Capturing lightning in a bottle wasn't as easy as Hawks had made it seem.

Santana

If *Sirocco* and *Bold Venture* were to prove anything but an artistic stretch, Santana did turn out one film that stood head and shoulders above all the others. Released in August 1950 and predating the disappointing *Sirocco*, *In a Lonely Place* told a different sort of story to those that were becoming Bogie's own personal treadmill. He gave himself the role of hot-tempered Dixon Steel, a struggling Hollywood screenwriter who just can't catch a break. Since he had become a leading man, Bogie's tough guys usually had a streak of humanity somewhere beneath their granite scowl, but the narcissistic Dix had no such saving grace.

After he is accused of a murder we know he didn't commit, Dix finds himself falling for his neighbour Laurel (Gloria Grahame), a down-on-her-luck actress who provides his alibi. With love comes inspiration and Dix is soon back to work, even as Laurel begins to fear his violent temper. Eventually the cops catch up with the killer, but there's no happy ending for Dix and Laurel, who Grahame captures perfectly. Instead, the film climaxes with the violent breakdown of the couple's relationship, when Dix almost throttles Laurel after he catches her packing to leave. It's far from a Hollywood ending.

116

Helmed by Nicholas Ray and very loosely adapted from Dorothy B. Hughes's novel by Andrew Solt, who restructured a faithful first screenplay by Edmund H. North, *In a Lonely Place* is a long way from the old Hollywood chestnut about a lost soul finding salvation through love. Though the ending of the movie is bleak, the original climax as written and shot was even more brutal. In this rejected finale, Dix kills Laurel moments before the police arrive to tell him that he's in the clear. Although Ray was partially responsible for conceiving this finale, he hated it even as it was being shot and knew that he had to come up with something else. Once shooting had wrapped for the day, he gathered Bogie, Grahame and co-star Art Smith and improvised a whole new ending. In a world that demanded neat conclusions, Ray left things open. It's up to us to decide what happens once Dix walks out of Laurel's apartment. He's a free man, but he nearly killed the one person who had tried to stand by him; it's not a happy ending, but it's a truly unforgettable piece of cinema.

Perhaps the sense of coiled tension present in every frame of the film was helped by the goings-on backstage. Bogie had never leveraged his star power to help Betty get a role and nor did she ask him to, but he believed that she was perfect for the part of Laurel Gray and wanted her on the picture. Once again, Jack Warner said no. Refusing to loan Betty out was a lesson in personal pique from the mogul, who was annoyed that Bogart's production company, Santana, was releasing its movies via Columbia, rather than his own studio. The casting spotlight then moved on to Ginger Rogers, but Ray requested that his wife, Gloria Grahame, also be considered. Ultimately, it was she who got the part.

This was not a case of jobs for the girls. In fact, Ray and Grahame's marriage was already in crisis when filming began and the movie finished it off. They were at such loggerheads that Grahame signed a contract promising that her husband was 'entitled to direct, control, advise and even instruct my actions during the hours from 9 AM to 6 PM every day except Sunday'. She even committed not to 'nag, cajole [or] tease' him for the duration of the increasingly tense shoot. The couple separated during filming and eventually divorced.

The movie wrapped on 1 December 1949, after five weeks of filming. When it was released the following year, critics celebrated *In a Lonely Place* as a welcome return to form for Bogie and lauded the knockout performance by Grahame, but the ending proved to be a sticking point. Ironically, it is the finale that has particularly withstood the test of time.

Happily ever afters were a Hollywood staple, but *In a Lonely Place* steadfastly refused to send audiences out of the cinema smiling.

On the page, Dix may not sound like too much of a stretch for Bogie, but there was one big difference that set this bad-tempered anti-hero apart. Dixon Steel was never redeemed, nor did he wish to be. In fact, he's a lost cause from the off. In a parallel with the man who played him, Dix is squarely from the right side of the tracks, but unlike Bogie he has failed to find his footing in Hollywood despite having every opportunity to do so. Bogie's demon was drink, whilst Dix's was his violent narcissism, and both had a conflicted relationship with the machinery of Tinseltown. Only Bogie had the self-awareness to just about make his peace with the business. Success helped, of course.

We see Dix at the lowest point of his career, desperate for a hit but thinking himself too good to give the moguls and the public what they want. Only when he's really on his uppers does Dix grudgingly agree to write a script based on a bestselling novel, albeit one that he considers himself too good to read. Instead, he hooks up with a hatcheck girl named Mildred, who is reading the potboiler that Dix wants to adapt. After she visits Dix's apartment to give him a detailed rundown of the novel's plot, he unceremoniously kicks her out. The next day, Mildred turns up dead.

There's nothing in any of this to suggest that Dix was a particularly testing part for Bogie. He's another world-weary, cynical guy, but what sets Dix apart is the fact that we suspect he's genuinely capable of committing the crime of which he's been wrongly accused. Laurel gives him an alibi, but the more she gets to know him, the more she comes to fear that she was wrong to trust Dix. They reach boiling point with a frantic car chase that ends with Dix viciously battering another driver into a pulp. By then, Laurel is desperate to escape.

Laurel accepts Dix's proposal not because she loves him, but because she's afraid of what he might do to her if she turns him down. When she finally attempts to flee, Dix turns on his lover in a murderous rage and strangles her. Though Dix stops himself just in time to take the telephone call that clears his name, it's already too late. Dix may not have murdered Mildred the hatcheck girl, but he has destroyed his one chance of redemption.

Bogie never raised a hand to Betty, but his temper was still there somewhere, and she caught a frightening glimpse of it during his drunken explosion on the yacht. Bogie could play Dix so well because he could recognise himself in the complex, tortured character. Perhaps that's why he always claimed to hate *In a Lonely Place*: it cut too close to the bone.

When *In a Lonely Place* was released, critics were united in praise of Bogie and Grahame. Bogie finally felt like they had recognised what he was capable of as an actor and he rode high on the plaudits. The same couldn't really be said for *The Enforcer*, which was released nationwide in February 1951. It would be Bogie's last film at Warners, the studio that had made him a superstar, and it was a far more by-the-numbers affair than *In a Lonely Place*.

The Enforcer saw Bogie take on one of his other stock characters, that of a hard-working attorney battling against the odds. It was a story ripped from the headlines, inspired by recent investigations into the contract killing organisation, Murder Inc. So far, so familiar, but what sets *The Enforcer* apart from the pack just a little is its unusual structure. The film unfolds as a series of flashbacks within flashbacks across three acts, giving Bogie ample opportunity to play both the desk jockey and a gun-toting hero, neither of which were much of a challenge. What it didn't offer was anything new; he could essay the hero or the anti-hero with ease, and *The Enforcer* asked him to do both.

Even though the film was released to reasonable reviews, Bogie didn't number himself amongst its fans. He greeted Santana's own *Sirocco* with the same disregard, explaining that 'I've been doing the role for years'. He was bored of the projects Warner imposed on him despite or because of his star power and frustrated by the admin created by his own Santana Productions. What Bogie needed was a maverick to ride in from left field and hand him the opportunity of a lifetime. In true Hollywood style, that's exactly what John Huston and producer Sam Spiegel did.

The African Queen

C. S. Forester's novel, *The African Queen*, had come close to realisation on more than one occasion, with names as diverse as Charles Laughton and David Niven thrown around for the role of the Cockney leading man. Though Warners had been sitting on the rights to the book, they'd shown no real interest in using it, so were happy to negotiate when Sam Spiegel came along and offered to take it off their hands. Spiegel nursed ambitious plans to shoot not on the backlot but in Africa, which was a bold move when it came to attracting finance. Luckily, Spiegel was a born wheeler-dealer. Through some shrewd and frankly risky dealings, he managed to get the cash in place.

In the Bogart marriage, Betty had always been the one with a wander-lust, whilst Bogie was content to stay at home: he had gone overseas only when the war dictated it and certainly never for fun. Whether a bachelor Bogie would have accepted John Huston's offer to play the lead in *The African Queen*, which would shoot in Africa before moving to England, was debatable, but he was caught in the spell of Huston and Spiegel and it seemed like too good an opportunity to turn down. He had one condition that had to be met: the Cockney would have to go. With Bogie unwilling to try his hand at accents, it was agreed that the part would be rewritten to lose the East End flavour. The deciding vote was cast by Betty, who was champing at the bit to travel beyond the US, even if her dreams were of Paris and Milan rather than a secluded film set in Africa. Once upon a time, Bogie would've turned it down flat and even now he wasn't willing to leave her at home and head off to Africa. Distance was what had killed his first two marriages, he was sure. Instead, he offered a compromise: if Betty would join him on the trip, he would treat her to a European holiday to remember around the shooting schedule. With about half the shoot taking place in the UK, it would be a perfect fit. Betty said yes.

Beyond occasional junkets to New York, this would be the couple's first real time away from little Steve, and Betty was torn. On the one hand, she knew that she would see her son again once shooting had wrapped, but on the other, that felt like a lifetime away. Ultimately, Bogie won the day: the couple would leave Steve with Alice Hartley and head for Africa. Sadly, things got off to a tragic start as soon as the Bogarts left. As they disappeared towards their gate at the airport after saying goodbye to family and friends, Alice suffered a fatal stroke.

Steve's faithful nurse, who had become a member of the family since she joined the household, collapsed at the airport as the Bogarts disappeared from view. She was still holding little Steve and only the swift intervention of another member of the party, who grabbed him as Alice fell, saved him from harm. Natalie stepped in to care for her grandson whilst a shortlist of trusted nurses was drawn up for Betty's urgent attention. Upon receiving the tragic news during her wait for a connecting flight, Betty's instinct was to go back. Instead, she allowed other voices to prevail and continued on her trip, satisfied that Steve was safe with Natalie.

This is, perhaps, the moment at which there is a temptation to judge Betty. Her son certainly did when he grew up to be a father. Rather than interview a new nurse from a phone booth in the lobby of the 21 Club in New York, it's natural to suggest that she should have turned around and gone straight back home. Bogie had no choice but to travel on to shoot *The African Queen*, but he didn't need Betty at his side. He wanted her there, and the two are very different.

Though as a younger man Steve told himself that he would've abandoned the trip, as he grew older and more reflective, he eventually made peace with Betty's decision and the decisions that led her to it. Bogie was a quarter of a century older than his wife and they wanted to grab every moment together they could. As far as they were concerned, Steve was in the very best hands, so there was no compelling reason to change their plans. Besides, wouldn't that just prove Bogie had been right all along about children coming between their parents? Or perhaps it would have taught him a hard lesson about what responsibility meant.

Betty rationalised her decision by telling herself that she had made a commitment to Bogie and the trip, but it's tantalising to wonder if there was something else at play too. The girl who had dreamed of being a star had seemingly been handed her success on a platter, along with her very own happy ending. However, in succumbing to that happy ending – with all its challenges and aggravations – she had lost sight of the very reason she had come to Hollywood in the first place. Betty Bacall had been overwhelmed by Betty Bogart, the famous man's wife. She hosted his dinner parties, charmed his friends and ran his household, but all of that took her further and further away from her own dream. By entrusting Steve's care to Natalie and continuing on to Africa, she was indulging Bogie's need to be her only priority, but she was resetting her own boundaries too. On this trip she would be Betty Bogart in private and Lauren Bacall, one half of a Hollywood power couple, in public. Yet every public outing reminded Betty of a hard truth: in the eyes of the world, she was Mrs Bogart first, and an actress second.

In Hollywood, stars were nothing special, but in Europe, Bogie was the focus of everybody's attention. Unlike Betty, Bogie had never cared for travel and now he was doing a lifetime's worth in the space of just a few short weeks, enduring the full glare of the spotlight everywhere he went. A whirlwind tour of Europe culminated with a private audience with the Pope in Rome, at which the Pontiff was noticeably struck by Betty. When they got back to their hotel that night, Bogie told his wife to stick close to the phone, ready to take the call when Pius XII rang to ask her out.

Shooting on *The African Queen* took place downriver from Ponthierville in the Belgian Congo, deep in the African jungle. Huston believed that the actors needed to really feel the hardships of jungle life if they were to communicate them to audiences, and that simply wasn't possible on the backlot. Though scenes in the water would be shot in the UK for health and safety reasons, for much of the time they were going to live the fiction. The cast and crew were lodged in bungalows of bamboo and palm leaves and Betty found herself in awe of her husband's self-possessed co-star, Katharine Hepburn. Hepburn was a much-needed voice of female reason on a shoot that was reigned over by Bogie and John Huston, long-time drinking buddies and more than a handful when the mood took them. As Spencer Tracy's partner, Hepburn had seen first hand the perils of booze, and as Tracy's long-time drinking buddy, Bogie was ready to be disapproved of. He turned into a schoolboy whenever Hepburn so much as rolled her eyes, mimicking her upper-class manner until she gave back just as good as she got. Her worldly resilience impressed the more sheltered Betty, who little realised at the time that she and Hepburn would form a lifelong bond during their trials in Africa.

Perhaps unsurprisingly for a man who never ventured out of the USA unless he absolutely had to, Bogie didn't enjoy the shoot and decided to give his inner curmudgeon free rein. When Huston and Hepburn went hunting together, Bogie forbade Betty to join them. He had suffered through his fair share of hunts alongside his father as a boy and instead preferred to stay at the campsite, compiling a mental list of all the things he hated about the place, from the heat to the insects to the food and everything in between. And that was before the titular *African Queen* sank and had to be rescued from the riverbed by hundreds of local workers. In a surprising contrast, Hepburn, whom Bogie had affectionately teased as an upper-class snob, revelled in the rough and ready shoot. One might reasonably have expected the apparently streetwise Bogie to take it on the chin whilst the genteel Miss Hepburn struggled, but not a bit of it.

With nothing else to do, Betty devoted herself once more to being a dutiful wife. Though she had resolved in America not to let her career fade into the shadows of domesticity, whilst Bogie was making *The African Queen*, she did just that. She made lunches for the crew and kept her little bungalow in perfect order, washing Bogie's socks and soothing his temper whenever he and Huston had one of their frequent disagreements. Though Betty was determined to return to her career, seeing her up to her elbows in washtub suds was exactly the picture of domestic bliss that Bogie had dreamed of. 'You think Baby would do this for me at home? Not on your life.' Little wonder that by the time they were home in Hollywood, Betty's sock-washing days were done.

However, as the arduous shoot went on and illness struck the camp, Betty increasingly pined for her little boy. Instead of watching Steve reach his milestones, she had spent four months playing nurse, cook and sock-washer in conditions that were at best inhospitable. It's little wonder that she had reached her limit.

With the exception of the perma-pickled Huston and Bogart, the cast and crew all suffered from one lurid tropical illness or another, and Hepburn was no exception. As the daughter of a urologist, the importance of staying hydrated had been drummed into her since childhood, so as her director and leading man served themselves Scotch from a lean-to bar, Hepburn chugged the bottled water that was provided on set. Unfortunately, the water she so virtuously drank was contaminated and she fell sick with serious digestive problems. Though the ever-professional Hepburn never took a day off to rest, she spent the time between takes vomiting and her weight plummeted. 'Those two undisciplined weaklings had so lined their insides with alcohol,' she said of Huston and Bogart, 'that no bug could live in the atmosphere.'[32] Hepburn's problems ended when she decided to drink only champagne instead. A true Hollywood ending.

As June drew on and the location shoot approached its end, Betty began to make plans for her reunion with Steve in London. Yet as she prepared for that happy meeting, news reached Africa that Mayo Methot had died. The divorce from Bogie had been the end of her Hollywood life and Mayo's efforts to restart her stage career in New York had been met with disinterest. Ever more dependent on alcohol, the ex-Mrs Bogart returned to her native Oregon and the care of her mother. Shortly before her death, Mayo had undergone surgery, which the press reported as the root of fatal complications. In fact, the cause of Mayo's death was alcoholism. Bogie took the news of his ex-wife's passing with his usual stoicism, mourning the fact that she had squandered her talent and her life. One cannot help but wonder whether he knew that he had come very close to doing exactly the same.

At first glance, the character of Charlie Allnut, the rough and ready steamboat captain who helms *The African Queen*, didn't seem like such a stretch for Bogie. It's a classic odd-couple tale as Charlie is thrown together with Katharine Hepburn's Rose Sayer, the upright sister of a British missionary. When she loses her brother to injuries suffered in an altercation with German soldiers who are raiding a nearby African village, Rose is left alone and apparently vulnerable in the mission house. Charlie, the rough and ready Canadian who delivers their supplies and minds his own business, comes by to play the unlikely white knight and carry her to safety, only to find the opinionated Rose taking over his life and his boat. She eventually ropes him into a plan to avenge her brother's death by destroying a German gunboat so British troops can mount a counter-invasion.

What brings *The African Queen* so vividly to life isn't only the master-stroke of filming on location, but the fact that the Hepburn–Bogart relationship seen on celluloid is not a million miles away from the real thing. At the start they are like people from different worlds, circling one another wearily, each sizing up the potential enemy. The set crackled with their mutual suspicions, but that animosity wouldn't last. As the shoot went on and they endured the shared hardships of life far from all of the luxuries of Hollywood, Bogie and Katie warmed to one another and became firm friends. The two actors shared an instinctive approach to their craft, delivering their lines not verbatim from the script but with all the spontaneity of a real conversation. They riffed on themes, overtalked one another and cut across the other's dialogue, improvising as they went. Some directors would have dragged back on the reins but Huston loved the energy that fizzed between his stars. The approach perfectly suited his own unconventional way of making movies, following his instincts rather than storyboards. Huston challenged the boundaries when he could, but he was sure to give *The African Queen* the sort of happy ending that befitted a light-hearted tale of adventure.

The African Queen opened to mostly great reviews, many of which focused not only on the scenery, but on Bogie and Hepburn's perfor-mances. Though Bogie might have appeared to have been playing a standard Bogart character, there was a playfulness about Charlie that his trench coat-clad cynics had all too often lacked. He handled the role with aplomb, and his first venture into adventure comedy was a resounding success.

The shoot had been a trial for everybody and when it ended, the Bogarts were soon on route to London to be reunited with their son. For three years, Betty had not been seen on screen at all and though she fully intended to return to her career, for now all she wanted was to see Steve again: work could wait. The family were reunited in London and Steve, by now more than able to chatter on to his parents, was as thrilled to see them as they were him. They spent the next six weeks in England, enjoying a diary packed with social engagements with everyone from the Oliviers to T. S. Eliot. Betty was in her element.

The African Queen gave Bogie exactly the sort of challenge he'd been dreaming of and when the Academy Awards came around, it seemed as though the Hollywood elite might finally agree. Betty was pregnant again when Bogie learned that he had been included in *The African Queen*'s clutch of Oscar nominations. His first foray into Technicolor looked set to be a knockout triumph.

Bogie had always professed that he had no interest in awards. He believed that the only way to truly decide the best actor was to have them all play the same role so they could be judged as equals. Since this was an impossibility, Bogie declared that it was all hooey. 'It's about time someone stuck a pin in the Oscar myth,' he told *Cosmopolitan* in 1950, 'and let out all that hot air contained in the Academy Awards.'[33] He had lost out for *The Petrified Forest* and *Casablanca* and was gracious in defeat, but even as he pontificated on the difficulties of judging and the overwhelming tendency to award dramatic roles rather than those in other genres, Bogie admitted that he'd be very happy to win an Oscar. If nothing else, 'It might be a nice item for my boy Stephen to throw at the neighbors' kids.'[34] As the boy who would one day crown Noël Coward with a silver tea tray, Bogart Junior had form for such mischief.

But that article had been penned twelve months before *The African Queen*, when Bogie had given up all hope of ever winning an Oscar for the by-the-numbers movies in which he was plying his trade. Though in public he greeted his nomination with his usual world-weariness, it's not too much of a stretch to imagine that in his heart, Bogie desperately wanted to win. He had struggled to gain recognition and more than paid his dues and, though the financial rewards had been huge, nobody knew more than Bogie that they had not been matched by artistic satisfaction. Despite its deprivations, *The African Queen* had given him just that, dragging him out of his comfort zone both geographically and artistically, and the result was a sparkling confection that has deservedly endured as a classic to this day. Yet Academy Awards aren't awarded on the strength of dues paid and Bogie, who never took anything for granted, was just one nomination amongst four. His greatest rival in a strong field was Marlon Brando, who added the nomination to a plethora of plaudits he had already received for *A Streetcar Named Desire*. It was the first of four consecutive Oscar nominations for Brando.

Though Betty desperately wanted Bogie to win, she had a secret fear that Brando might pip him to the winning post. In the event, as the history of cinema tells, the victory went to Bogie. On that warm Hollywood night, he forgot his grumbling cynicism to give a heartfelt and joyous acceptance speech. He paid tribute to the crew, singling out Spiegel, Hepburn and Huston for particular praise. And nobody cheered louder than Betty. 'I thought I'd have the baby then and there,'[35] she recalled later.

Holmby Hills

As the excitement from Oscar night died down, the family were on the move. Though Bogie never asked for more than his own little den and a boat out on the ocean, Betty loved the trappings of stardom and the couple's new Beverly Hills pad at 232 South Mapleton Drive in Holmby Hills gave her all that in spades. This stunning French Colonial mansion had more than a dozen rooms, along with the Hollywood must-haves of a swimming pool – added by the Bogarts for their children – tennis court and plenty of space for a collection of expensive cars. At the heart of the house was what became known as 'the Butternut Room', a sumptuous wood-panelled study where the couple hosted their friends around a well-stocked bar. It was to be Bogie and Betty's last home together.

Bogie and Betty's second child was a daughter, born just after midnight on 22 August 1952. The little girl was named Leslie Howard Bogart in honour of the friend who had come through for Bogie when *The Petrified Forest* went to Hollywood. Howard had been lost at sea in 1943 when the plane in which he was travelling was shot down, but Bogie never forgot the debt he owed to his buddy. He had kept his word when it mattered most, a rarity in the dream factory. Leslie's name was Bogie's very personal tribute.

Though Betty loved being a wife and mother – she particularly enjoyed watching Bogie getting to know his new daughter – other avenues were beginning to command her attention. Despite having a new contract from Fox, she was no closer to being back on screen, and had instead taken a rather left-field interest in politics. Or one particular politician, at least.

Bogie had been stung by politics in 1941 when he led a march to Washington to protest against the actions of the Un-American Activities Commission. When the gesture saw him labelled a Communist, he bristled and declared that he was one thing and one thing alone: a patriotic American. The incident never left him and he advised Betty to think again

126

about whether she wanted to nail her colours to the mast. She went against Bogie's advice and joined the campaign for Adlai Stevenson with a fervour that she admitted many years later had bordered on obsession. Despite himself, Bogie went along on the campaign trail to play the supportive husband to his wife, coming out for the politician she freely confessed that she worshipped. Stevenson wasn't a romantic threat to Bogie, but he knew from bitter experience that dabbling in politics could cause an actor plenty of problems.

Betty reflected decades later that she had let herself become almost overwhelmed by Adlai Stevenson and the belief that, through him, she might make a difference to the world. There was no romantic intrigue, even if Betty had been quietly indulging one of her crushes, but there was plenty of mutual flirting and an infatuation born out of her own relative immaturity. Still only in her 20s, Betty had begun to feel subsumed into the roles of wife and mother and Stevenson recognised her other talents, something everybody else seemed to miss. Though Stevenson was defeated at the polls, Betty had relished the cut and thrust of politics and learned that there was a whole world outside of Hollywood.

Bogie usually let Betty's crushes pass, but her fascination for Stevenson concerned him not because he had a rival, but because he didn't want his wife's idealism to lead her into trouble. He was less concerned by a 1953 article she wrote for *Look* magazine, entitled 'I Hate Young Men', in which she catalogued all of the older men who had captured her eye. She was at pains to point out that these weren't men whose looks and charm had won her over, nor her crushes, but gents who simply fascinated her. It included the likes of John Huston and, of course, Adlai Stevenson, and Bogie read it with affectionate indulgence. After all, she never blinked an eyelid at the close friendships he enjoyed with two of his former wives.

Perhaps it's telling that, despite her political awakening, Betty's next move was to return to work. She had striven for her career only to put it on hold to start a family, and had been ready to go back before the cameras for a long time. And this time, she was going to choose her own project. After hearing about a play by Zoe Akins named *The Greeks Had a Word for It* from George Cukor, Betty told Darryl F. Zanuck that she wanted a part in the movie adaptation. Having never played comedy before, Zanuck informed Betty that she would have to make a screentest, her first since those early days with Hawks. Though Zanuck passed it off as a mere for-mality, Betty was put out even as she knew she had to agree. She aced the test and got the part: Lauren Bacall was coming back to the movies as one of the stars of *How to Marry a Millionaire*, as the play was retitled for Hollywood. It would be directed by Jean Negulesco, another man who fascinated her.

Until now pigeonholed as a vamp to varying degrees of success, *How to Marry a Millionaire* gave Betty the chance to show that she could do more than smoulder. The only fly in the ointment was the fact that whilst she was shooting in Hollywood, Bogie was slated to be in Italy filming *Beat the Devil*, and Betty had planned to be with him. It was a choice that would have enormous repercussions, for it was unlikely that Betty would ever get another chance like this one. If she squandered it for the sake of a trip to Europe at her man's side, she might as well kiss her career goodbye. Betty didn't know which way to turn, so she asked her husband for his advice. No longer fearing that time apart might sound the death knell for his marriage and well aware of what the role meant to her, Bogie urged her to take the movie and get back to work.

How to Marry a Millionaire

As Schatze Page in *How to Marry a Millionaire*, Betty sparkled in a knock-about comedy about three gals on the lookout for rich husbands. It was the first time that Betty and Bogie had really been apart and, perhaps surprisingly given their intense romance, Betty revelled in it. She'd forgotten how much she enjoyed being an actress in Hollywood, where the backlots bustled. Life as a wife and mother had its joys, but acting had been her dream for as long as she could remember.

Produced by Nunnally Johnson – one of the men included on Betty's list of fascinating chaps – from his own screenplay, *How to Marry a Millionaire* wasn't going to win any awards for originality. But this candyfloss-light movie provided charm in spades, and it did it in CinemaScope and blazing Technicolor. New York had arguably never looked better on screen than it did in the hands of director Jean Negulesco and, freed from the chains of vampishness, Betty sparkled. As one of a trio of unashamed gold diggers, she was happy to mine her classy, smouldering New Yorker image for laughs as the apparently streetwise girl who almost rejects an honest but poor 'gas pump jockey' for his millionaire father, until a last-minute change of heart at the altar. As her two best friends abandon their gold-digging ways for more humble men, the three gals and their spouses drink a toast to true love. It's only then that Schatze learns that her new gas pump jockey husband, played by Cameron Mitchell, is even more wealthy than his father. She got her millionaire after all.

Co-starring with Betty Grable and Marilyn Monroe, one might expect Betty to have had a few tales to tell, but the shoot was a happy one. In fact, it reminded Betty of her early days in the theatre, a memory that invigorated her personally and it shows in her performance. The technical limitations of CinemaScope meant that scenes had to be shot in long takes, with the actors moving through the long, narrow screen space to make full use of the process. It was more like acting for the stage than the screen, and since the theatre remained Betty's first love despite her having been tempted to Hollywood, she revelled in it. It was a real knockout cast too, giving Betty the opportunity to star alongside Betty Grable, already a veteran performer despite only being in her 30s, and Marilyn Monroe. However, Marilyn was a different sort of player altogether.

How to Marry a Millionaire was to be Marilyn's third feature release of 1953. Along with *Niagara* and *Gentlemen Prefer Blondes*, it cemented Monroe as a sex symbol and one of the most bankable female stars in the world. Stories abound of Marilyn's crippling struggles with timekeeping, her personal troubles and her own self-confidence, and these eventually led to the shutdown of her last film, 1962's *Something's Got to Give*, in which she co-starred with Dean Martin. A decade before that, though, those problems were already evident on the set of *How to Marry a Millionaire*.

Marilyn was frequently late for her calls and when she did appear, she was shadowed at every turn by her personal acting coach, Natasha Lytess. Originally the head coach at Columbia Pictures, Lytess had been introduced to Marilyn when she was signed to the studio in 1948 and she soon made herself indispensable. She remained Monroe's personal coach until 1956, when Marilyn dismissed the overbearing Lytess from her position. By that time, the coach controlled her superstar charge like a sergeant major.

During shooting on *How to Marry a Millionaire*, however, Lytess was the only person Marilyn trusted and she sought her coach's approval of every take before she would move on to the next. If Lytess believed that her charge could improve, a scene would be shot and reshot, take after take, until she finally gave the nod. Nobody else got a look in. Recognising how isolated their co-star was becoming, the two Betties resolved to make Marilyn feel more comfortable. They went out of their way to befriend her as much as they could despite Lytess's constant presence, but it was an uphill struggle. Betty suspected that Marilyn envied her marriage and family and the security that came with it, but she was never really able to get to know her co-star on anything beyond a superficial level. Unlike her warm friendship with Katharine Hepburn, Betty's relationship with Marilyn Monroe never flourished into anything more than a tentative, pleasant acquaintance.

Whilst Betty was enjoying herself in a Technicolor world of romance and ditzy comedy, Bogie embarked on a project of an entirely different sort. John Huston had come across Claud Cockburn's pseudonymous novel, *Beat the Devil*, in Ireland, and he saw a movie in it. As a former member of the British Communist Party, Cockburn was all too aware that the political climate was getting a little too hot when the novel was published in 1951, so he took the pen name James Helvick to avoid any pushback. *Beat the Devil* was a rip-roaring thriller that was to be Huston and Bogie's next – and last – collaboration, so long as Huston could convince his leading man to pony up $10,000 for the rights. By the time the novel came out, the impoverished Cockburn was on his uppers and Huston's desire to purchase the rights was as much a favour to an Irish neighbour as it was an artistic decision. Bogie agreed that Santana would pitch in the cash, but he drew the line at casting Betty in a central role. This wasn't a project for her.

'I read your insidious and immoral proposals to my wife,' he admonished Huston in a comically angry letter addressed to 'Dear Fly in the Ointment'. 'I therefore instructed Miss Bacall to disregard your blandishments, and as your employer I request you not to further fuck up my home, which has already been fucked up by Adlai Stevenson.' The role of Maria, Bogie's onscreen wife, went to Gina Lollobrigida, whilst Jennifer Jones was cast as Gwendolen, his mistress. It's difficult, once seen, to imagine Betty replacing either.

When Bogie learned that Huston planned to shoot in black and white, he counselled his friend to reconsider. Black and white was a dying process, he warned, and would damage the movie's prospects not only at the cinema, but on television in years to come. Huston disagreed but, since it was Bogie's money on the line, left the final decision to him. Bogie went with Huston's instinct and agreed to black and white.

The bigger problem with *Beat the Devil* was the script itself. Claud Cockburn's initial efforts at adapting his own novel for the screen had left Huston and Bogie lukewarm, and they brought in Tony Veiller and Peter Viertel, who worked with Huston on *Moulin Rouge* and *The African Queen* respectively, to do extensive rewrites. Unfortunately, the rewrites just made things worse and left the star grumpily questioning whether the film was a drama, a comedy or even an action movie. With time pressing and shooting scheduled to begin in less than a week, Jennifer Jones's mogul husband, David O. Selznick, suggested that Huston press the nuclear button and bring in the big guns to get the project off the ground. Truman Capote was residing in Rome and Selznick assured Huston that he'd be able to whip the screenplay into shape. He had done just that for Selznick's *Indiscretions of an American Wife*, which had recently wrapped in Rome. What they hadn't banked on was Capote insisting on a phone conversation with his pet raven in Rome every single day. If the raven ever refused to speak, Capote delayed production to make a visit to see the bird in person.

Bogie had found the initial tone of the movie confusing, but it eventually coalesced into a comedy adventure co-starring such considerable talents as Robert Morley and Peter Lorre, with everyone apparently having a high old time. Sadly, it didn't necessarily translate to the audience. *Beat the Devil* tells the story of Billy Dannreuther – Bogie – a rich American fallen on hard times who joins a criminal conspiracy to acquire land in British East Africa that is rich with Uranium deposits. So far, so simple, but it soon becomes a lot more complicated as murder and double cross get in the way of what should be a nice little earner.

Though Betty didn't appear in *Beat the Devil*, she had plans to head to Ravello in Italy and join her husband the moment *How to Marry a Millionaire* wrapped. In the event, fate conspired to eventually shift the reunion to London, three long months after the couple had last seen one another. If Betty had been happy for a while to moon after Adlai Stevenson and enjoy a version of the single life, all of that was forgotten as soon as she laid eyes on her husband again. Nearly a decade down the line, Betty and Bogie hadn't lost their spark.

From *Caine* to *Contessa*

When *Beat the Devil* came out, it bombed. Jack Warner dismissed it as a folly, saying 'I think they shot it through beer-bottle-glass,' and the public tended to agree. Even Bogie sniffed that 'only phonies like it', little suspecting that it would one day be regarded as a cult favourite. The following year, though, Bogie was back on form with a couple of solid-gold classics and an intriguing teardown of the Hollywood machine: *The Caine Mutiny*, *Sabrina*, and *The Barefoot Contessa*. Though the critics didn't necessarily hold them all in high regard, time has seen the trio placed in the pantheon of Bogie's most popular performances. Betty's own comeback in

How to Marry a Millionaire had been a resounding triumph and at home, life was good. She'd finally escaped the vamps and proved that Betty Bacall and light comedy were a winning combination. Bogie, meanwhile, was looking for a challenge of his own.

What makes the combination of *Caine*, *Sabrina*, and *Contessa* so intriguing for the potential future direction of Bogie's career, had it not been so tragically curtailed, is the fact that none of them is what we would necessarily regard as a typical Bogart role. Unlike some that he had been landed with and those that he had been suspended over, *The Caine Mutiny* was that rare thing: a movie that Bogie desperately wanted to make. From the start, Columbia and producer Stanley Kramer wanted Bogie for the picture, but they leveraged his obvious hunger to barter him down from his customary $200,000 salary. They got a bargain, even if it left their star to complain 'this never happens to Cary Grant'.

Based on the novel by Herman Wouk, *The Caine Mutiny* tells the story of the USS *Caine*, a minesweeper in World War II that has recently been placed under the command of hardline disciplinarian, Lieutenant Commander Queeg. As Queeg's behaviour grows increasingly more bizarre, including instituting strip searches to find out who stole some strawberries from the officers' mess, the crew begin to suspect that their captain is mentally unstable. Eventually Queeg abandons an escort mission and fatefully ignores the pleas of Lieutenant Maryk, played by Van Johnson, to change course in order to avoid a typhoon. With the men urging Maryk to seize command before Queeg's behaviour ends in catastrophe, he leads a mutiny to save the ship.

Central to all of this is the lurking presence of Fred MacMurray as self-serving Lieutenant Tom Keefer, who has witnessed all of Queeg's erratic and paranoid behaviour. However, at the very moment when the men have a chance to alert senior naval personnel to Queeg's tyranny and possibly avoid the otherwise inevitable mutiny, Keefer's refusal to speak out against the captain forces the hand of his reluctant comrades. When Maryk and his fellow officers are eventually placed under court-martial for the mutiny, Keefer once again betrays them and falsely testifies that Queeg was a robust, skilful commander. With Keefer's lies threatening to send the officers to prison, it is only Queeg's breakdown on the witness stand that convinces the court-martial to clear the men of mutiny.

At the heart of a stellar cast, Bogie's performance as the crumbling victim of combat stress is masterful. From commanding captain to twitchy paranoiac, to his eventual collapse, Queeg is no comic-book villain nor a wide-eyed grand guignol madman. Bogie had been through tough times himself and was able to mine the character's humanity, as well as his crumbling mental health under the onslaught of extreme stress and battle fatigue. Perhaps, in his way, he understood Queeg better than most.

The Caine Mutiny was directed by Edward Dmytryk, one of the so-called Hollywood Ten who were sentenced to prison following their testimony to the House Un-American Activities Committee. Dmytryk, who had been a member of the Communist Party for just one year, was dismissed from his contract at RKO and fled for the UK. He returned to America in 1951 to testify again – this time naming names – and begin his slow Hollywood comeback.

Bogie himself had history with the Hollywood Ten, as he had been one of the members of the Committee for the First Amendment back in 1947. This liberal collection of actors came together under the organisational team of screenwriter Phillip Dunne, actress Myrna Loy and directors John Huston and William Wyler, with the intention of protesting against the actions of the House Un-American Activities Committee. Believing that there were no Communists amongst their number nor amongst the Hollywood Ten, Bogie and Betty naively neglected to do any due diligence and were horrified to learn that their belief was mistaken: the fallout for their careers could be devastating. Bogie tried to undo the perceived damage to his reputation with a 1948 *Photoplay* article entitled 'I'm No Communist', which instead caused a backlash from those who believed he'd sold out his friends for the sake of his billing. But that was never Bogie's style: whatever else he might have been, he was a scrupulously honest man. When he said he wasn't a Communist, he meant it. Bogie wasn't the type to name names.

As a member of the Committee for the First Amendment, Bogie felt as though he'd been duped into supporting a cause that was very different to the one he'd signed up to, and backpedalled his way out of it as quickly as he possibly could. In 1947, it wasn't enough to forestall furious letters from fans, but his career had survived. Against the odds, so had Dmytryk's, but it would take *The Caine Mutiny* to truly prove he had made it back from the brink of oblivion.

The Caine Mutiny deservedly became the second highest-grossing movie of 1954 and was showered with nominations and plaudits, including another Oscar nod for Bogie. In a film bristling with jaw-dropping performances, his study of Queeg is nothing short of spectacular, whether essaying his tyrannical reign or his tattered nerves as he faces the court.

As *Time* so memorably put it in an issue that featured an illustration of the star as Queeg on the cover, 'he deliberately gives Queeg the mannerisms and appearance of an officer of sternness and decision, then gradually discloses him as a man who is bottling up a scream.' *The Hollywood Reporter* hailed Bogart's performance as 'a high point in the history of screen acting', leaving the man who professed not to care what the critics thought beaming – or beaming as much as he ever did, anyway.

The success of *The Caine Mutiny* chased away the lingering ghost of *Beat the Devil*'s failure, not only for critics and audiences, but crucially for Bogie too. It didn't clinch him a second Oscar, though; instead, he lost out to Marlon Brando's knockout performance in *On the Waterfront*. But the award would only have been a garnish for Bogie: he had wanted the role more than any trophy, and he had aced it. In his quest to push his own boundaries and keep that battered trench coat from seeing the light of another day, Bogie followed up the hard-hitting psychological tale with a light romantic comedy. Secure and celebrated, he was in the mood to spread his wings.

Billy Wilder had big plans for his next Paramount production, *Sabrina*. It told the comical love story of Linus Larrabee, a financier who wins the heart of his chauffeur's daughter, Sabrina Fairchild, and Wilder had earmarked Cary Grant for the lead role opposite Audrey Hepburn. With Grant unavailable and the role still going begging just a week before shooting was due to begin, Wilder decided to take a leap in the dark and cast a man who had never been considered for the Cary Grant roles: Humphrey Bogart. Bogie had performed in comedic parts before, most notably showing off his whipcrack smarts in *The African Queen*, but this was a different matter altogether. It was a return to the flannels and delightful drawing rooms of those early stage outings decades earlier, and it was not the sort of character anyone expected from Humphrey Bogart, least of all the man himself.

Sabrina is as light as gossamer and utterly charming with it. When her schoolgirl crush on David, the playboy son of the family, goes unrequited, young Sabrina attempts suicide. She is rescued by Linus, David's bookish brother, and sent off to Paris to finish her schooling and heal her broken heart. Sabrina returns as a sophisticated, attractive young lady, so when David sees her, he's naturally smitten at first sight.

The trouble is, David is already engaged, and his fiancée's father possesses the power to block an enormous corporate deal and ruin the Larrabees. Determined to avert disaster, Linus befriends Sabrina with the intention of seeing her safely back on the boat and out of harm's way. It won't come as a surprise to hear that the odd couple fall in love. After a great deal of angst, some derring-do and plenty of laughs, David comes to his senses, the business deal and his engagement are both saved and Linus and Sabrina sail for Paris and their very own unlikely happy ever after.

Just as *The Caine Mutiny* benefited from a smash-hit Broadway fore-runner, Bogie was familiar with *Sabrina* from its runaway Broadway pro-duction, *Sabrina Fair*, but he had certainly never considered it as a possible vehicle for himself. When Wilder and co-writer Ernest Lehman made a personal approach to the star, they didn't even have a finished script and Bogie was far from impressed to learn that he was second choice to the otherwise indisposed Grant. It wasn't something that happened often. Sensing his reticence, Wilder promised Bogie that he'd guide him through these unchartered waters. He'd enjoy it, Wilder assured him.

Two things convinced Bogie to say yes; one was the encouragement of his agent, Sam Jaffe, who urged him to stake a claim to romcoms now he'd more than proved his point when it came to drama. The other was a very hefty pay packet. It was particularly generous compared to that of co-star William Holden, who played Bogie's bleached-blond brother and love rival, David. 'Bogart gets the girl,' said Wilder wryly, 'because he's getting three [actually two] hundred thousand for the picture, and Holden is getting a hundred and a quarter.'[36]

Bogie might be getting the big bucks, which he'd sacrificed for his dream role in *The Caine Mutiny*, but money had never been his motivation and he soon regretted it. The shoot was anything but the frothy comedy seen on screen and tension fizzed from start to finish. Bogie resented being second choice right from the off so when shooting began and the script still wasn't finalised, it didn't exactly leave the star brimming with confidence. New pages were being delivered every day and when shooting wrapped each evening, Holden, Hepburn and Wilder would convene in Holden's dressing room for a private drinks party to which Bogie wasn't invited. What made matters worse was the fact that, despite his intention never to use his stardom to help Betty, Bogie had rather liked the idea of seeing her in the title role. It was never anything but a remote possi-bility, and it's impossible to imagine anyone other than Audrey Hepburn as the gamine Sabrina.

Every evening, when Bogie arrived home, he was grumbling about his co-stars. Holden and Hepburn had both picked up Oscars the previous year,[37] and Audrey was the toast of the town, but Bogie wasn't about to cut her any slack. When Hepburn forgot her lines, he chastised her for spending time partying with Holden rather than studying; he positively relished being able to play the wise old owl, disapproving of the youthful follies he perceived. Since Hepburn received another Oscar nomination for her role in the film, it's worth noting that the Academy clearly didn't share his reservations. Things reached a head when Bogie prepared to shoot a scene with Holden only to learn that he didn't have the most up-to-date script pages, because Lehman had mistakenly only given them to Hepburn, Holden and Wilder. Usually the consummate professional, Bogie stormed off set and forced a break in production. Knowing that Wilder had just seven weeks to bring the film in, his walkout was a powerful protest.

It wasn't Bogie's first movie with Holden, and the two men had butted heads when they shared the screen in 1939's *Invisible Stripes*. After Bogie had made unflattering comments about his co-star, Holden took every opportunity he could find to stick the knife in; by the time of *Sabrina* Holden had moved on, but his very presence irked Bogie. He'd taken those dressing room parties to heart, choosing to forget that he preferred to head home to his family at the end of each day. Even during location shooting in New York, Bogie insisted on stopping at 6.00 pm sharp, as his contract stipulated, so he could return to the St Regis Hotel, where Betty was waiting to hear his complaints. It didn't matter that he was getting paid more, nor that he got the girl: Bogie was determined to be annoyed.

All that mattered to Bogart was that he didn't like the way things were going, and nothing could change that. The atmosphere on set became increasingly toxic once Bogie learned that Holden – a married man – was having an affair with the much younger Hepburn. Of course, Bogie had plenty of form himself when it came to fooling around with a young co-star, but the Holden/Hepburn intrigue riled him to a ridiculous degree. A man's private life was his own business, but when it had a negative impact on the shoot, it became Bogie's business too. Basically, Audrey annoyed Bogie simply because she wasn't Betty.

Having thrown himself into the role of Queeg body and soul, the lurch into comedy was proving a challenge for Bogie, and he had begun drinking again in order to endure the unhappy *Sabrina* shoot. Just as Howard Hawks had bitterly threatened to send Betty into obscurity at Monogram back at the start of her career, Bogie now made similarly cutting remarks to Wilder and was happy to tell the press that the movie wasn't his cup of tea. Yet when the moment came for the cameras to roll, Bogie was there with his lines learned and his performance polished. It was a miserable but surprisingly efficient way of making a movie.

Bogie decried the script as 'a crock of shit' and railed against the absurdity of a man like him winning a girl like Audrey, perhaps forgetting that he had done just that in real life. He clashed with Wilder again and again, claiming that he couldn't understand the director's Viennese accent and constantly berating him about every aspect of the movie. Wilder, meanwhile, grew to hate his star and then, conversely, to admire him. The two men had nothing in common whatsoever, but Wilder respected a professional above all things, and Bogie was never more professional than when he wanted to make a point about how unprofessional his peers were. When Bogie had taken the role, he had been open with Wilder about his doubts over the unfinished script and the director had promised that he'd make it a happy experience. He had done no such thing. In the scant years left to Bogie, he and Wilder put their animosity behind them and developed a civil if not exactly effusive relationship; they never ventured onto the same movie set again.

Despite the tensions on set, none of them show on the screen. *Sabrina* charmed the public and critics alike and Bogie, just as his friends had expected, was hailed for this new comical string to his bow. Lately, though, he had begun to be inconvenienced by an irritating cough, which seemed to be getting progressively worse. After a lifetime of hard living, Bogie dismissed it as an occupational hazard, but as he prepared to travel to Rome to work on Joseph L. Mankiewicz's *The Barefoot Contessa* alongside Ava Gardner, he was already experiencing the early symptoms of what would prove to be a fatal disease.

Mankiewicz had sealed his place in the pantheon of greats in 1950 when *All About Eve*, which he directed from a script co-written with Mary Orr, won six Academy Awards. *The Barefoot Contessa* would not repeat that feat. The film is a rags-to-riches biography of 'the world's most beautiful animal', the recently murdered and entirely fictional Spanish leading lady Maria Vargas, who had risen from destitution to royalty. Many people wrongly believed that the inspiration for the picture had been provided by Gardner herself but in fact the character's story was far closer to that of Rita Hayworth, *aka* Gilda. Born Margarito Cansino, she had been discovered as a dancer in Mexico and reached giddy and not always happy heights before her marriage to Prince Aly Khan. Though her story didn't end in murder, it had more than its share of tragedy.

Bogie signed on to play Harry Dawes, a has-been movie director trying to kick a booze habit for the umpteenth time. It might not seem like new territory, but it was another change of pace after *Sabrina*'s light comedy and heavy atmosphere. Unfortunately, Bogie once again took issue with his leading lady's love life and let it mar their on-set relationship. Gardner had recently separated from Frank Sinatra, who would become a good friend of the Bogarts and eventually Bacall's fiancé – though never her husband – and she was enjoying a love affair with matador Luis Miguel Dominguin. Why Bogie cared was anyone's guess, but he liked to remind her that 'half the world's female population would throw themselves at Frank's feet, and here you are flouncing around with guys who wear capes and little ballerina slippers.' You could never say he wasn't loyal to his buddies.

Even before Bogie started, Gardner was feeling the strain of carrying a film that would stand or fall on her performance. 'When I arrived in Rome early in 1954, I was nervous at being in such high-toned company,' she later admitted. 'And I have to say that Mr Bogart did not make my life any easier.' Mr Bogart, never particularly pampering when it came to his co-stars, was getting ever more irascible.

Beat the Devil, *The Caine Mutiny* and *Sabrina* all gave Bogie a chance to do something a little different, but *The Barefoot Contessa* was more familiar ground. It is a big, showy soap opera, haunted by the ghost of *All About Eve* but still inarguably entertaining. That Bogie's seen-it-all-before turn will surprise nobody isn't necessarily a criticism; he is a solid presence in a solid movie, but he could have played the role in his sleep.

If Bogie's world-weariness on screen was the product of the life he'd lived off it, Betty's sophisticated exterior belied her naivety. She still wanted to please, and she proved that in an incident that occurred when she visited Bogie in Rome during filming on *The Barefoot Contessa*. Frank Sinatra asked her to deliver a coconut cake to his estranged wife, Ava Gardner, in the hope of winning her back. Not wanting to let Frank down, Betty took the cake with her as hand luggage from New York to London and on to Rome, where Bogie told his co-star that she should make arrangements to collect it. Miss Gardner did no such thing, saddling Betty with the unwanted and increasingly not-very-fresh confectionary. Rather than simply ditch the cake, Betty stormed onto the lot and hammered on the door of Ava's dressing room. The handover passed off without a word of thanks and a sullen Mrs Sinatra wouldn't even take the box, gesturing instead for the furious Betty to put it on a table and skedaddle. Years later, after her own ill-fated engagement to Ol' Blue Eyes, Betty had a little more sympathy for Ava's dismissal of Frank's gift.

We're No Angels

Bogie played up his hard man image to comic effect in 1955's *We're No Angels*, as one of three escaped convicts seeking a hiding place with a family in French Guiana on Christmas Eve. Unlike another escaped convict he would play later that year in *The Desperate Hours*, Frenchman Joseph and his friends, played by Aldo Ray and Peter Ustinov, experience their very own Christmas miracle. Along with their pet snake, Adolphe, the trio restore the family's struggling shop, play Cupid for the daughter and even indulge in a little DIY. Then, having decided that prison is infinitely preferable to the world outside, they head back to jail to finish their sentences. As the film ends and they settle down to sleep, each of the men – and Adolphe, of course – earn their very own halo.

We're No Angels was yet another adaptation of a stage play but, unlike *Sabrina*, it wasn't a box office smash. Nor was *The Left Hand of God*, which followed it. Reuniting Bogie with Edward Dmytryk, the film saw him star as a downed airman masquerading as a priest in order to escape the clutches of Lee J. Cobb, improbably cast as a Chinese warlord. Perhaps the most notable thing about *The Left Hand of God* was the casting of Gene Tierney as the obligatory love interest. Tierney had been battling manic depression, and her career had been badly affected by those struggles. It seemed likely that she and Bogie, the consummate professional who didn't suffer perceived fools gladly, would not be a happy match.

Instead, the opposite happened. Though Tierney had only recently been discharged from a stay in residential care and was far from well, Darryl F. Zanuck wanted her for the picture. Bogie had the right of veto written into his contract, but he didn't exercise it; perhaps he remembered the plight of his sister, Pat, not to mention Mayo's troubles. Not only did Bogie okay Tierney as his co-star, but he did all he could to ease her through the shoot as smoothly as possible. He proved to be anything but the irascible curmudgeon who had chastised Audrey Hepburn and was instead the friend that Gene Tierney needed. She never forgot that 'his patience and understanding carried me through the film'.[38]

Betty, meanwhile, had not been idle. Having proved her adept hand at comedy with Jean Negulesco's *How to Marry a Millionaire*, she returned to dramatic roles in 1954 with Negulesco's *Woman's World*, joining an ensemble cast headed by Clifton Webb and June Alyson. In a solid but unremarkable movie, Betty played a supportive wife struggling to hold onto her workaholic husband, Fred MacMurray. She followed it in 1955 with *The Cobweb*, a turgid drama set in a psychiatric hospital under the rule of *Confidential Agent*'s Charles Boyer's alcoholic, disturbed doctor. Sadly for Betty, whilst Bogie was picking up the sort of projects that topped the charts, *The Cobweb* was the opposite. It bombed at the box office, losing MGM more than $1 million. She just couldn't score a hit.

Bacall's next film, *Blood Alley*, fared little better. Though Betty enjoyed the experience of working with John Wayne on this propaganda piece about Americans helping Chinese villagers escape to Hong Kong, the film attracted little interest from moviegoers. Bogie had been asked to star but his price was too high and the film is probably most notable for the presence of Sweden's Anita Ekberg, who won a Golden Globe as Most Promising Newcomer for her role as Wei Ling. It was 1955.

Domestic Bliss

Things couldn't have been going better on the domestic front for the Bogart family. They were settled and happy in their Beverly Hills home and Betty was realising her dream of travelling too. She was present in London for Queen Elizabeth II's coronation and was finally living the life she wanted again, a whirlwind combination of wife, mother and movie star. From pool parties in Las Vegas with Noël Coward to sailing trips with the kids and long, lazy days at home, the Bogarts had achieved a happiness that Bogie had never known and that Betty had dreamed of. She revelled in her role as wife and mother and guests were always welcome at their home. Almost.

> We had a kind of endless open house. Our friends knew the rule: If the light was on over the front door, that meant we were awake and they were welcome to stop in for a drink. If the light was out, forget it. We had the light on quite often. It was a terrific house – a very friendly, open, easy home.[39]

Bogie and Betty were the leader and den mother of the Holmby Hills Rat Pack, a loose collection of stars and drinking buddies who were as close as America came to royalty. Among the members of the group were Judy Garland and her husband Sidney Luft, David Niven, Swifty Lazar, Hepburn and Tracy, Cary Grant and, of course, Frank Sinatra. When Bogie died, it was Frank who assumed his throne as the head of the pack and later formed his own Summit – better known as the Rat Pack – with

Dean Martin, Sammy Davis Jr, Peter Lawford and Joey Bishop. Betty's career was on the up too and she was personally invited by Noël Coward to take the lead opposite him in a television production of *Blithe Spirit*, an opportunity she relished. She had also been offered a lead role in Douglas Sirk's *Written on the Wind*, a glorious soap opera of a movie that would star Rock Hudson, Robert Stack and Dorothy Malone. Betty's CV needed a shot in the arm and though *Blithe Spirit* gave her a sense of enormous self-satisfaction, she pinned all her Hollywood hopes on *Written on the Wind*. Once again though, she found herself outshone as Dorothy Malone commanded the picture with a firecracker performance that clinched her an Academy Award.

Once Bogie had shied away from publicity, but now he was a family man, he was even happy to invite television cameras in for a look around their Holmby Hills sanctuary. There was a hint of trouble in paradise when neighbours on South Mapleton Drive filed a lawsuit regarding the Bogarts' barking dogs, but there was little else to trouble the harmonious marriage – not even Betty's crush on Adlai Stevenson and a new fascination for Leonard Bernstein, who bewitched her at first sight. 'You'd probably have a great time for a weekend,' was Bogie's wry observation about his wife's infatuation. 'But not for a lifetime.'

Bogie knew that Betty's career was stagnating, so when NBC approached the couple with an offer to star together in a live television production of *The Petrified Forest* under the Producer's Showcase strand, he broke his own rule about not doing TV. Bogie had no interest in signing up to the project, but he knew that Betty could use the exposure. The play had to be considerably shortened for television and Bogie was more than happy to sacrifice his own lines, not least because his cough was becoming more debilitating than ever. Though the telecast could not capture the magic of the movie nor that first electrifying stage performance all those years ago, audiences and critics loved it. It was Bogie's one and only appearance in a live television drama, and he nailed it.

Though he had only taken the role so Betty could get the Bette Davis part, it was Bogie who pulled down the best notices. Offered a whole host of lucrative television projects in the wake of *The Petrified Forest*, he rejected them all. He had no interest in a TV career and for one fan at least, that was exactly how it should be.

Cheers for Bogart and Bacall – for deciding that they are really film stars and not wanting to do big things on TV ... I consider that this is being loyal to picturegoers, who have put them where they are. – Mary Giles (Mrs.), Banbury, Oxon.[40]

Bogie had found running Santana a headache, but he now formed a new company in a distribution deal with Allied Artists. Mapleton Pictures would seek out the very best roles for one man: Humphrey Bogart. Even better, it'd likely provide some good scripts for Betty too. And she needed them.

The Cough

In the last phase of his career, Bogie left behind the tough guys in favour of a variety of different types, but he was back on more familiar ground for *The Desperate Hours*. In his penultimate movie, Bogie would play a shadowy and dangerous escaped criminal holding a family hostage. The film was based on a play which was in turn, based on a true story, and the role Bogie was slated to play had been originated on stage by Paul Newman. It was essentially a return to Duke Mantee – as Bogie himself acknowledged – older, but no wiser.

Just before *The Desperate Hours* opened in autumn 1955, Bogie mentioned casually to Betty that he'd been at lunch with Greer Garson when he had been seized by a coughing spasm. Concerned by what she heard, Garson took him to see Dr Maynard Brandsma to get a full examination. Brandsma saw nothing untoward in an initial course of X-rays, but suggested the star reduce his alcohol and tobacco intake whilst he waited for the results of sputum tests. The very fact that Bogie had consented to see a doctor was a sign that he suspected there was something seriously wrong, but he pushed the ongoing tests out of his mind and encouraged Betty to do the same. Of more importance to the couple was the prospect of working together again, with a reunion planned in Mapleton and Warner Bros' planned movie adaptation of *Melville Goodwin, USA*, a sweeping rale of love and war.

In many ways, going back to Warners for wardrobe and make-up tests was like going home. The lot was familiar and the personnel old friends, and it had been too long since Bogie and Betty had appeared on the big screen together. There was a magic to the movies that television simply didn't have and the Bogarts were raring to get in front of the cameras and recapture the old lightning in a bottle.

First, though, Bogie wanted to wrap on what he didn't know would be his last film. Fittingly, *The Harder They Fall* was a noir, with Bogie playing

Eddie Willis, PR man to a crooked boxing promoter. It was during the shooting of *The Harder They Fall* that Bogie learned the full extent of his illness: his cough was a symptom of oesophageal cancer. The diagnosis was devastating, but Bogie kept right on going, just as he had through every trial and tribulation of his life. Determined to fight, he kept his illness a secret and turned in a pitch-perfect performance as the luckless Eddie, who has nothing left to rely on but his own moral code. Playing opposite method actor Rod Steiger caused Bogie headaches galore and the two men never got along, but still Bogie didn't let it distract him from the job in hand: he put everything into his performance as Eddie Wilkes, perhaps knowing deep down that it would be the last part he ever played. Steiger later reminisced about the shoot, on which nobody but Bogie knew what he was facing. 'Once [Bogie] didn't like one or two scenes because he had "a watery look in his eye",' he wrote. 'I don't know if it was because it was his last film or tears of pain.' Yet Bogie pushed on, determined to finish the movie before he faced the uncertain future.

All of Bogie and Betty's plans came to a shuddering halt with his illness. Further tests showed that the tumour needed to be operated on immediately, yet Bogie's instinctive reaction was to say no, citing the cost to the studio if shooting on his next picture was delayed. Dr Brandsma countered that it would cost them a lot more if he didn't, because any delay would mean death. Bogie faced the diagnosis with his usual stoicism, Betty with stunned confusion. By the time they left the doctor's office, the operation was in the diary for the following week, and Bogie was in the hands of pioneering surgeon John Jones, one of the very best in the business. Bogie's operation would be significant; Jones would open the actor's chest via his ribcage and remove the diseased tissue, then connect what little would remain directly to his jejunum, the small intestine that attaches to the stomach. It was a blessing that they had caught it so early, said the cautiously optimistic doctors.

When the Bogarts got home that evening, everything had changed. They sat down with Stephen and Leslie and explained that their father was unwell. Of course, they downplayed the severity of Bogart's illness and said instead that he would be going away for a couple of weeks to have an operation on his throat. When he came home, they assured the youngsters, it would be business as usual.

That weekend, the couple went to Frank Sinatra's house with members of the Holmby Hills Rat Pack and broke the bad news. For the rest of the weekend and the rest of Bogie's life, Sinatra ensured that the focus was all on his beloved friend. When Bogie was in his last weeks and couldn't leave the house, Sinatra visited virtually every day, cementing his bond with the Bogarts. He would prove to be one of Bogie's most devoted champions in his final days. 'I think we're parent substitutes for him or something,' Bogie teased, but he knew that Sinatra's love for him ran deep. There was no handwringing or tears because that wasn't their style; instead it was laughter, booze and easy friendship. Even though his friends and family knew the full story, the press were told only that Bogie was undergoing surgery to remove a swelling in his throat. It was a strictly need-to-know basis, but woe betide anyone who suggested that Bogie was ashamed or embarrassed by his frailty. 'Why should I [be ashamed]?' he asked. 'It's a respectable disease – nothing to be ashamed of, like something I might have had.'

As Bogie and Betty travelled to the hospital on 22 February 1956 to prepare for the operation at 7.00 am the following day, the couple held hands. With a wry smile, Bogie observed, 'Funny, I've never spent much time with doctors. Now I'll probably spend the rest of my life with then.' Betty knew that her husband's joke was a smokescreen for his fears, but she chuckled amiably and clung on tighter. There was nothing else they could do.

Bogie was in surgery for ten long hours, leaving Betty to wait anxiously for his return. During the operation, it was discovered that the cancer had spread into his lymph nodes, which the surgeons removed in an effort to halt its progress. It was the most devastating outcome imaginable and the prognosis for the future looked more bleak than ever. Yet Betty painted on a brave face for her reunion with her anaesthetised husband that same night. Somehow, she kept up the act for the ten months that followed, wavering only when a violent bout of coughing tore open his healing stitches. On that occasion, Betty raised the alarm and saved the day.

A Slight Malignancy

Over the days that followed, Bogie was slowly eased back into the land of the living. His weight plummeted and he endured gruelling radiation treatment that went on for weeks, an ordeal that left him ever more debilitated. Yet as cards, gifts and even chef-prepared food poured in, Bogie faced his agony with fortitude. On one memorable occasion, when Bogie had hobbled to the bathroom, John Huston snuck in and hid under his bedclothes, waiting for him to return. Such silliness was just the tonic Bogie needed.

Yet there was a secret that Betty knew and Bogie did not. With the progression of the cancer into her husband's lymph nodes, the prognosis had become near terminal. Betty kept the secret because she simply couldn't accept it. 'I could not think in terms of Bogie not living,' she admitted later, so she thrust the idea of it from her mind. Instead, she encouraged his dreams of returning to work with a movie entitled *The Good Shepherd* and together they nursed plans for *Melville Goodwin, USA*, which Bogie was still determined would reunite them onscreen. He didn't speak in terms of if, but when.

By the time he got home, Bogie was learning to eat again with his newly reconstructed throat. Despite his diagnosis, he continued to smoke: his only concession was to switch to filtered cigarettes and cut down to one pack a day. Ordered to rest, Bogie took to his bed with his dog, Harvey, faithfully at his side. Leslie and Stephen were thrilled to see their father again and slowly, bit by bit, Bogie even grew strong enough to spend time on the *Santana*. It was a moment he had dreamed of, but he could no longer endure the energetic excursions he had once undertaken and was content to sit peacefully in calm waters.

Though Betty couldn't think of going back to work, when she was offered a plum role opposite Gregory Peck in *Designing Women*, Bogie told her to take it. Grace Kelly had vied with Betty for the role, believing it had been written just for her, but ultimately Betty won out. The set would become her sanctuary from the sadness at home and a place where she could, for a little while at least, forget what the future held. *Designing Women* would eventually be regarded as one of Betty's best movies; as she noted later with her characteristic dry wit, '[Grace] got the prince, I got the part.'

As Betty prepared for the shoot, Bogie and 7-year-old Stephen even took the *Santana* out for a weekend trip, from which Bogie returned with a new spring in his step. The only thing that darkened his mood was a false press report by gossip columnist Dorothy Kilgallen – for whom Frank Sinatra nursed a particular loathing – that placed Bogie in the non-existent Memorial Hospital, literally on his deathbed.

For Bogie, who was beginning to feel better after so long, it was like a punch to the gut. Quite apart from the fact that there was no Memorial Hospital in Los Angeles, the entire story was fiction. He had fought the battle of his life over the past few months and needed to vent. He did so in a furious rejoinder to the *Journal-American*, the paper that had printed Kilgallen's piece, and any other press outlet that wanted to publish it too.

I have been greatly disturbed lately at the many unchecked and baseless rumours being tossed to the people among you regarding the state of my health. To set the record straight, as they say in Washington (and I have as much right to say this as anybody in Washington has), a great deal of what has been printed has had nothing to do with the true facts. It may be even necessary for me to send out a truth team to follow you all around.

I have read that both lungs have been removed, that I couldn't live another half-hour; that I was fighting for my life in a hospital which doesn't exist out here; that my heart has stopped and been replaced by an old gasoline pump from a defunct Standard Oil station. I have been on the way to practically every cemetery you can name from here to the Mississippi – including several where I am certain they only accept dogs. All the above upsets my friends, not to mention the insurance companies. So, as they also say in Washington, let's get the facts to the American people – and here they are.

I had a slight malignancy in my esophagus. So that some of you won't have to go into the research department, it's the pipe that runs from your throat to your stomach. The operation for the removal of the malignancy was successful, although it was touch and go for a while whether the malignancy or I would survive.

As they also say in Washington, I'm a better man than I ever was – and all I need now is about thirty pounds in weight, which I am sure some of you could spare. Possibly we could start something like a Weight Bank for Bogart and believe me, I'm not particular which part of your anatomy it comes from.

In closing, any time you want to run a little medical bulletin on me, just pick up the phone and, as they say in the Old Country – I'm in the book.

Not long after he penned his letter, Bogie started to suffer from pains in his left shoulder. At first, his doctors dismissed the new symptoms as a pinched nerve, but when he began to lose weight and painkillers no longer eased the agony, Bogie was readmitted to hospital. This time, the doctors informed Betty that she should prepare herself for bad news: the cancer might have returned, and nitrogen mustard was the only hope if it had. Reeling from the warning, Betty agreed that Bogie should be told only that the surgery would correct some troublesome scar tissue pressing down on the nerve. It was a white lie intended to keep his morale up.

We cannot know whether Bogie suspected the truth, but he dutifully packed up some detective novels, a bottle of whisky and a small chess set and went back to St John's Hospital. This time, the treatment didn't work. When Bogie came home after this procedure, he was weaker than ever and had to submit to what he considered the ultimate indignity: a nurse. Sadly for Betty, though *Written on the Wind* did give her the hit she needed, it came as Bogie was entering the final stages of his life. And though the movie made millions, it was Dorothy Malone and Robert Stack who caught the eye of the Academy; studio politics meant that Bob didn't win, but Dorothy did.

Betty was a constant presence at her agonised husband's side as he declined, fighting with her entire being to keep him comfortable and, most importantly, alive. She was barely glimpsed outside the house for weeks, devoting her every moment to meeting his needs. When asked why it was that Betty never went into town anymore, Bogie replied, 'She's my wife and my nurse. So she stays home. Maybe that's the way you tell the ladies from the broads in this town.'

Bogie was almost permanently confined to his room by now, with visitors strictly regimented and timetabled to give him time to move to the Butternut Room to receive them. Even his children were banned from his room and Bogie tried to see them as little as possible, desperate to spare them the memory of his suffering. He remembered too well watching his father's decline all those years ago, so all but Bogie's most trusted confidantes were denied access to the bedroom where he had to spend most of his days. He was so weak that he had to be carried by the nurse up and downstairs, an arrangement that the actor complained about until a dumbwaiter was transformed into a rough and ready elevator to carry him from his bedroom to the place where he would meet his friends. At five o'clock everyday, Betty and Auerlio Salazar, the family's gardener, would help Bogie dress before Salazar lifted him carefully onto a stool in the dumbwaiter. He would then meet his employer on the ground floor and help him into the wheelchair that he had to use to get around.

Bogie found the whole ordeal humiliating, but once he reached the Butternut Room, he was back to being Bogie. Ready with a cigarette and a cocktail, he waited to receive his visitors and, mindful that their time with him might be growing short, his buddies came by every single evening. When some friends, most notably rat packer Swifty Lazar, stopped visiting at all, Bogie accepted their decision without resentment. He shrugged off their absence, and played it cool as only Bogie could.

Through all of it, Betty was her husband's defender and champion. Some of Bogie's steel had rubbed off on his wife, but as Bogie turned 57 that Christmas, even she was forced to confront the truth. The nitrogen mustard, Bogie's last chance for recovery, had not worked and all hope was lost. Now it was a matter of weeks, not months. Little had been said to Bogie of his impending death, but he was an intelligent man, and he knew better than anyone what the future held. He had fought all his life and had finally come up against an unbeatable opponent. It was a resigned Bogie who told Betty with characteristic pragmatism, 'I guess I'm a goner.'

And still the friends came, loving as ever and grieving for the man who had seemed eternal. 'Before we left I kissed him good night, the way I always did, and Spencer put a hand on Bogie's shoulder,' Katharine Hepburn told Stephen Bogart. 'Bogie gave him one of those great Bogart smiles, you know, and he said, "Good-bye, Spence," but those words, Stephen, they were so filled with meaning. You knew Bogie meant it as a final good-bye, because your father had always said good night in the past, not good-bye.'[41] Tracy would later be so consumed by grief that he was too distressed to deliver the eulogy at his treasured friend's funeral.

That night, Betty and Bogie watched *Anchors Aweigh* together in Bogie's bed. The following morning, as she left to collect the children from Sunday school, Bogie saw Betty off with his final words, 'Goodbye, kid.' In later years, the press would combine this with Hepburn's story to suggest that Bogie had known that he was going to die that day. Betty, ever the pragmatist after years with the man who made pragmatism his life's work, dismissed that as nothing but a hokey story. Bogie always said goodbye when she left the house, she shrugged, there was nothing remarkable about that morning.

By the time Betty reached home, Bogie was in a coma. He had fought to the last. Humphrey Bogart died in the early hours of 14 January 1957. Never one for the trappings of stardom, his simple funeral was attended by some of the most famous names in showbiz. Thousands of people lined the streets outside All Saints Episcopal Church in Beverly Hills and the lots at Warner Bros and 20th Century Fox stood silent for one minute of remembrance. Standing before the altar, which was decorated with a model of the *Santana*, John Huston delivered a eulogy to a remarkable man: 'He is quite irreplaceable. There will never be another like him.'

Bogie was cremated. He had wanted his ashes to be scattered over the Pacific from the *Santana*, but legal quibbles meant that they would have to be buried instead. Bogie's ashes were interred at Forest Lawn Memorial Park, with the little gold whistle charm that he had given Betty before they were Mr and Mrs Bogart. 'If two people love each other there can be no happy ending,' Betty lamented. 'Since one dies before the other.'[42] Yet in some ways, the couple were immortal.

Me and Mrs Me

The day-to-day story of Betty and Bogie ended with Humphrey Bogart's death, but Betty's story went on. She told it herself in her memoir, *By Myself*, from her romance with Sinatra to a second marriage to Jason Robards Jr, and her triumphs and setbacks, both professional and personal. Betty had to wait until 1981 to headline a movie and when it came, *The Fan* was far from a classic. But, like her late husband, Lauren Bacall became an icon. As outspoken and forthright as Bogie had been, Betty was one of the few actors still working in the twenty-first century deserving of the title legend; she was deservedly recognised by the Academy with an Honorary Award in 2010. Lauren Bacall, born Betty Joan Perske, died on 12 August 2014, nearly seventy years after she had married Humphrey Bogart.

To the end, Betty and Bogie were remembered as two halves of one whole. Betty moved on with life, raising her children and learning to go on without the man she had loved, but she never forgot Humphrey Bogart, who had been such a fundamental part of her life. Bogart and Bacall endure, forever golden in the mind of the public and the too-few remarkable movies they shared.

Decades later, Betty reminisced:

The pictures I have in my head from those early years are very clear, ... whatever it was, it was most definitely the match made in heaven.[43]

Notes

Act One: Bogart

1. Hyatt Downing, 'End of the Rainbow for Bogart', *Screenland*, vol. 50, issue 5, March 1946, p. 92.
2. Kate Holliday, 'I Can't Say I Loved Her', *McCall's*, vol. 76, issue 10, July 1949, p. 30.
3. David Niven, *Bring on the Empty Horses*. New York: Putnam (1975), p. 237.
4. Howard Sharpe, 'The Amorous Life Story of a Movie Killer', *Movieland*, vol. 1, issue 2, March 1943, p. 33.
5. Kate Holliday, 'I Can't Say I Loved Her', *McCall's*, vol. 76, issue 10, July 1949, p. 8.
6. Jonah Ruddy and Jonathan Hill, *Bogey: The Man, the Actor, the Legend*. New York: Tower (1965), p. 15.
7. Clifford McCarty, 'Humphrey Bogart', *Films in Review*, vol. 8, issue 5, May 1957, p. 193.
8. David Niven, *Bring on the Empty Horses*. New York: Putnam (1975), p. 237.
9. A. M. Sperber and Eric Lax, *Bogart*. London: Phoenix (1998), p. 31.
10. Ibid., p. 34.
11. Howard Sharpe, 'The Amorous Life Story of a Movie Killer', *Movieland*, vol. 1, issue 1, February 1943, p. 33.
12. Ibee, 'Meet the Wife', *Variety*, vol. 73, issue 2, 29 November 1923, p. 18.
13. Eliza Miller Lenz, 'Humphrey Bogart Learned Business Side of Theater Before Becoming Actor', *The Billboard*, vol. 36, issue 29, 19 July 1924, p. 20.
14. Ibid.
15. Ibid.
16. Grace Mack, 'Meeting Up with a New Menacing Man', *Motion Picture*, vol. 52, issue 6, January 1937, p. 88.
17. Peter Bogdanovich, 'Bogie in Excelsis', *Esquire*, vol. 63, issue 3, 1 September 1964, p. 178.
18. 'Woman Who "Shocked America"', *The Daily Mail*, 15 August 1927, p. 3.
19. 'Broken Romance', *The Daily Mail*, 14 November 1927, p. 11.
20. 'Actress Seeks Divorce', *Evening Star*, issue 30,510, 12 November 1927, p. 22.
21. Nathaniel Benchley, *Humphrey Bogart*. Boston: Little, Brown & Company (1975), p. 39.
22. Mori, 'The Skyrocket', *Variety*, vol. 94, issue 1, 16 January 1929, p. 55.
23. *Screen Book*, vol. 6, issue 22, January 1940, p. 66.
24. Kate Holliday, 'I Can't Say I Loved Her', *McCall's*, vol. 76, issue 10, July 1949, p. 32.
25. Arthur Hopkins, *Reference Point*. New York: Samuel French Ltd. (1948), p. 62.
26. Ibid.

27. George Benjamin, 'Bad Boy Makes Good', *Modern Screen*, vol. 22, issue 1, December 1940, p. 32.
28. Eugene Burr, 'The Petrified Forest', *The Billboard*, vol. 47, issue 3, 19 January 1935, p. 18.
29. George Frazier, 'Close-Up: Humphrey Bogart', *Life*, vol. 16, issue 24, 12 June 1944, p. 72.
30. 'Bogart's Beard', *Variety*, vol. 117, issue 5, 15 January 1935, p. 53.
31. 'Grapewin's "Forest"', *Variety*, vol. 120, issue 1, 18 September 1935, p. 3.
32. 'Bogart in Pic, Too', *Variety*, vol. 120, issue 4, 9 October 1935, p. 3.
33. George Benjamin, 'Bad Boy Makes Good', *Modern Screen*, vol. 22, issue 1, December 1940, p. 71.
34. Ibid.
35. Ibid.
36. Kate Holliday, 'I Can't Say I Loved Her', *McCall's*, vol. 76, issue 10, July 1949, p. 32.
37. Marriages, *Variety*, vol. 131, issue 11, 24 August 1938, p. 54.
38. Howard Sharpe, 'The Amorous Life Story of a Movie Killer', *Movieland*, vol. 1, issue 2, March 1943, p. 33.
39. Patricia Clary, 'Boyer Mum; Bogart, Too', *Detroit Evening Times*, 12 August 1945.
40. Thornton Delehanty, 'The Battling Bogarts', *Photoplay, Combined with Movie Mirror*, vol. 22, issue 4, March 1943, p. 31.
41. Erskine Johnson, 'In Hollywood', *The Monitor-Leader*, vol. 84, issue 134, 9 November 1944, p. 6.
42. George Frazier, 'Close-Up: Humphrey Bogart', *Life*, vol. 16, issue 24, 12 June 1944, p. 59.
43. George Benjamin, 'Bad Boy Makes Good', *Life*, vol. 22, issue 1, 11 December 1940, p. 71.
44. Ibid.
45. Walt, 'The Maltese Falcon', *Variety*, vol. 144, issue 4, 1 October 1941, p. 9.
46. Hyatt Downing, 'End of the Rainbow for Bogart', *Screenland*, vol. 50, issue 5, March 1946, p. 90.
47. George Benjamin, 'Bad Boy Makes Good', *Modern Screen*, vol. 22, issue 1, December 1940, p. 71.
48. 'Bogart Lives Up to His Promise', *Picturegoer*, vol. 11, issue 564, 3 October 1942, p. 11.
49. John Huston, *An Open Book*. London: Columbus Books Ltd. (1988), p. 114.
50. Erskine Johnson, 'In Hollywood', *Imperial Valley Press*, vol. 42, issue 235, 11 August 1944, p. 2.
51. 'WB's Starlet List', *Variety*, vol. 156, issue 3, 27 September 1944, p. 11.

Act Two: Bacall

1. David Lewing, 'Not For Me the World of Fake and Phoney Love Affairs', *Daily Mail*, issue 23982, 3 July 1973, p. 12.
2. David Thomson, 'Lauren Bacall: The souring of a Hollywood legend', *Independent*, 11 September 2004. www.independent.co.uk/news/people/profiles/lauren-bacall-the-souring-of-a-hollywood-legend-545780.html (accessed June 2023).
3. George Jean Nathan, 'First Nights & Passing Judgments', *Esquire*, 1 July 1942, p. 91.

4. W. Austin Brodie, 'Out-of-Town Openings', *The Billboard*, vol. 54, issue 41, 10 October 1942, p. 9.
5. Thanks to the involvement of William Faulkner on screenwriting duties and Ernest Hemingway having written the original novel, *To Have and Have Not* remains the only film narrative on which two winners of the Nobel Prize for Literature have been employed.
6. Matt Tyrnauer, 'To Have and Have Not', *Vanity Fair*, 10 February 2011. www.vanityfair.com/news/2011/03/lauren-bacall-201103 (accessed June 2023).
7. Lauren Bacall, *By Myself and Then Some*. New York: HodderEntertainment (2005), p. 91.
8. W. H. Mooring, 'At Least She's Worth Shouting About', *Picturegoer*, vol. 14, issue 625, 3 February 1945, p. 6.
9. Peter Bogdanovich, *Who the Devil Made Do It*. New York: Alfred A. Knopf (1997), p. 328.
10. Robin Brantley, 'What Makes a Star? – Howard Hawks Knew Best of All', *The New York Times*, 22 January 1978, p. 11.
11. Lauren Bacall, *By Myself and Then Some*. New York: HodderEntertainment (2005), p. 101.
12. Ken Smith, 'Bogey Cried at Our Wedding', *Picturegoer*, vol. 29, issue 1038, 26 March 1955, p. 14.

Act Three: Bogie and Baby

1. Lauren Bacall, *By Myself and Then Some*. New York: HodderEntertainment (2005), p. 107.
2. Thornton Delehanty, 'Bogie and his Slim', *Photoplay*, vol. 27, issue 2, July 1945, p. 34.
3. Lauren Bacall, *By Myself and Then Some*. New York: HodderEntertainment (2005), p. 113.
4. Walter Winchell, 'Walter Winchell: On Broadway', *Detroit Evening Times*, 28 December 1944, p. C-11.
5. 'Bogarts Fight to the Finish', *The Wilmington Morning Star*, 20 October 1944, p. 12.
6. 'Bogart and Wife Ready to Break', *The Waterbury Democrat*, vol. 62, issue 282, 4 December 1944, p. 1.
7. Robin Brantley, 'What Makes a Star? – Howard Hawks Knew Best of All', *The New York Times*, 22 January 1978, p. 11.
8. Harold Heffernan, 'Looking Back on 1944 – and Ahead Through 1945', *The Sunday Star*, vol. 2074, issue 36,767, 31 December 1944, p. B-8.
9. Jack Ashland, 'B and B', *Photoplay*, vol. 27, issue 5, October 1945, p. 95.
10. Dotson Rader, 'Be Open to Whatever Happens', *The Times News: Parade*, vol. 92, issue 138, 18 May 1997, p. 5.
11. 'Humphrey Bogart Admits Lauren Bacall Romance', *Imperial Valley Press*, vol. 43, issue 94, 25 January 1945, p. 5.
12. Don Iddon, 'Don Iddon's Diary', *Daily Mail*, issue 15,214, 7 February 1945, p. 2.
13. Dotson Rader, 'Be Open to Whatever Happens', *The Times News: Parade*, vol. 92, issue 138, 18 May 1947, p. 6.
14. Ibid., p. 5.

15. Thornton Delehanty, 'The Battling Bogarts', *Photoplay, Combined with Movie Mirror*, vol. 22, issue 4, March 1943, p. 76.
16. 'Paging Hollywood', *Essex Newsman*, 26 August 1947, p. 2.
17. 'Bride Learns', *Detroit Evening Times*, 3 October 1945, p. 18-C.
18. Hyatt Downing, 'End of the Rainbow for Bogart', *Screenland*, vol. 50, issue 5, March 1946, p. 89.
19. Kahn, 'Confidential Agent', *Variety*, vol. 160, issue 9, 7 November 1945, p. 25.
20. Graham Greene, *Yours etc.* London: Reinhardt Books (1989), p. 188.
21. Humphrey Bogart, 'In Defense of My Wife', *Photoplay*, vol. 29, issue 1, June 1946, p. 99.
22. Jack Ashland, 'B&B', *Photoplay*, vol. 27, issue 5, October 1945, p. 95.
23. Ibid.
24. 'Hot from Hollywood', *Screenland*, vol. 50, issue 4, February 1946, p. 6.
25. Jack Ashland, 'B&B', *Photoplay*, vol. 27, issue 5, October 1945, p. 96.
26. Peter Bogdanovich, *Who the Devil Made Do It*. New York: Alfred A. Knopf (1997), p. 336.
27. Bosley Crowther, 'The Screen', *The New York Times*, 24 August 1946.
28. Lloyd Sheard, 'Bogart and Bacall: Here's How They Fooled Hollywood', *St Louis Post-Dispatch*, vol. 78, issue 28, 29 January 1956, p. 18.
29. Ibid.
30. 'Letters to the Editor', *Time*, 8 November 1948.
31. 'Bogey-Man to Public Relations', *Variety*, vol. 176, issue 4, 5 October 1949, p. 9.
32. Katharine Hepburn, *The Making of the African Queen, or, How I Went to Africa with Bogart, Bacall, and Huston and Almost Lost My Mind*. New York: Knopf (1987), p. 118.
33. Humphrey Bogart, 'The Oscar Myth', *Cosmopolitan*, vol. 128, issue 3, March 1950, p. 31.
34. Ibid., p. 165.
35. Lauren Bacall, *By Myself and Then Some*. New York: HodderEntertainment (2005), p. 220.
36. Bob Thomas, *Golden Boy: The Untold Story of William Holden*. New York, St Martin's Press (1983), p. 85.
37. Holden won an Oscar for *Stalag 17* and Hepburn for *Roman Holiday*.
38. Gene Tierney, with Mickey Herskowitz, *Self-Portrait*. New York: Wyden (1979), p. 164.
39. Curtiss Anderson, 'Lauren Bacall at 50', *McCalls*, vol. 102, issue 5, February 1975, p. 48.
40. 'Thanks Bogie and Betty', *Picturegoer*, vol. 30, issue 1059, 20 August 1955, p. 26.
41. Stephen Bogart and Gary Provost, *Bogart: In Search of My Father*. Belmont: Untreed Reads (2012).
42. Curtiss Anderson, 'Lauren Bacall at 50'. *McCalls*, vol. 102, issue 5, February 1975, p. 48.
43. Lauren Bacall, *By Myself and Then Some*. New York: HodderEntertainment (2005), p. 501.

Bibliography

Bacall, Lauren, *By Myself and Then Some* (New York: HodderEntertainment, 2005).

Barbour, Alan G., *Humphrey Bogart* (London: W.H. Allen & Co, Ltd, 1974).

Behlmer, Rudy, *Inside Warner Bros. (1935–1951)* (New York: Viking Press, 1985).

Benchley, Nathaniel, *Humphrey Bogart* (Boston: Little, Brown & Company, 1975).

Berg, Scott A., *Kate Remembered: Katharine Hepburn, A Personal Biography* (London: Simon & Schuster UK Ltd, 2003).

Bogart, Stephen and Provost, Gary, *Bogart: In Search of My Father* (Belmont: Untreed Reads, 2012).

Bogdanovich, Peter, *Who the Devil Made Do It* (New York: Alfred A. Knopf, 1997).

Choppa, Karen, *Maud Humphrey: Her Permanent Imprint on American Illustration* (Atglen: Schiffer Publishing Ltd, 1997).

Christopher, Nicholas, *Somewhere in the Night: Film Noir and the American City* (New York: Henry Holt and Company, Inc, 1997).

Crowe, Cameron, *Conversations with Wilder* (New York: Alfred A. Knopf, 2001).

Cunningham, Ernest W., *The Ultimate Bogart* (Los Angeles: Renaissance Books, 1999).

Curtis, James, *Spencer Tracy: A Biography* (London: Hutchinson, 2011).

Ebert, Roger, *Roger Ebert's Book of Film: From Tolstoy to Tarantino, The Finest Writing From a Century of Film* (New York: W.W. Norton & Company, Inc., 1997).

Gardner, Ava, *Ava: My Story* (New York: Bantam, 1990).

Greene, Graham, *Yours etc.* (London: Reinhardt Books, 1989).

Grobel, Lawrence, *The Hustons* (New York: Charles Scribner's Sons, 1989).

Harmetz, Aljean, *Round Up the Usual Suspects: The Making of Casablanca* (New York: Hyperion, 1992).

Hepburn, Katharine, *The Making of the African Queen, or, How I Went to Africa with Bogart, Bacall, and Huston and Almost Lost My Mind* (New York: Alfred A. Knopf, 1987).

Hepburn, Katharine, *Me: Stories of My Life* (New York: Alfred A. Knopf, 1991).

Hirschhorn, Clive, *The Warner Bros. Story* (London: Octopus, 1986).

Hopkins, Arthur, *Reference Point* (New York: Samuel French Ltd, 1948).

Hopp, Glenn, *Billy Wilder: The Cinema of Wit, 1906–2002* (Los Angeles: Taschen, 2003).

Huston, John, *An Open Book* (London: Columbus Books Ltd, 1988).

Hyams, Joe, *Bogart & Bacall: A Love Story* (New York: David McKay Company, Inc, 1975).

Hyams, Joe, *Bogie: The Biography of Humphrey Bogart* (New York: The New American Library, 1966).

Johnson, Kevin, *The Dark Page* (New Castle: Oak Knoll Press, 2007).

Kanfer, Stefan, *Tough Without a Gun: The Extraordinary Life of Humphrey Bogart* (London: Faber, 2010).

Kidd, Charles, *Debrett Goes to Hollywood* (New York: St Martin's Press, 1986).

McBride, Joseph (ed.), *Focus on Howard Hawks* (Englewood Cliffs: Prentice-Hall, Inc., 1972).

McCarthy, Todd, *Howard Hawks: The Grey Fox of Hollywood* (New York: Grove Press, 1997).

Meyers, Jeffrey C., *Bogart: A Life in Hollywood* (Boston: Houghton Mifflin, 1997).

Meyers, Jeffrey C., *John Huston: Courage and Art* (New York: Crown Archetype, 2011).

Niven, David, *Bring on the Empty Horses* (New York: Putnam, 1975).

Paris, Barry, *Audrey Hepburn* (New York: Berkley Books, 2001).

Quirk, Lawrence J., *Lauren Bacall: Her Films and Career* (Secaucus: Citadel Press, 1986).

Robertson, James C., *The Casablanca Man: The Cinema of Michael Curtiz* (London: Routledge, 1993).

Ruddy, Jonah and Hill, Jonathan, *Bogey: The Man, the Actor, the Legend* (New York: Tower, 1965).

Schatz, Thomas, *The Genius of the System: Hollywood Filmmaking in the Studio Era* (New York: Pantheon Books, 1989).

Server, Lee, *Ava Gardner: Love is Nothing* (New York: Macmillan, 2006).

Sperber, A. M. and Lax, Eric, *Bogart* (London: Phoenix, 1998).

Spoto, Donald, *Enchantment: The Life of Audrey Hepburn* (London: Hutchinson, 2006).

Spoto, Donald, *Marilyn Monroe: The Biography* (London: Chatto & Windus, 1993).

Thomas, Bob, *Clown Prince of Hollywood: The Antic Life and Times of Jack L. Warner* (New York: McGraw-Hill Publishing Company, 1990).

Thomas, Bob, *Golden Boy: The Untold Story of William Holden* (New York, St Martin's Press, 1993).

Thompson, Verita, *Bogie and Me: A Love Story* (London: W.H. Allen & Co, Ltd., 1983).

Tierney, Gene, with Mickey Herskowitz, *Self-Portrait* (New York: Peter Wyden, 1979).

Warner, Jack and Jennings, Dean, *My First Hundred Years in Hollywood: An Autobiography* (New York: Random Books, 1964).

Warner Sperling, Cass and Millner, Cork, with Warner Jr, Jack, *Hollywood Be Thy Name: The Warner Brothers Story* (Rocklin: Prime Publishing, 1994).

Widdicombe, Toby, *A Reader's Guide to Raymond Chandler* (Westport: Greenwood, 2001).

Wood, Robin, *Howard Hawks* (New York: Doubleday, 1968).

Zolotow, Maurice, *Billy Wilder in Hollywood* (New York: Limelight Editions, 1987).

Websites

The following archives played a crucial part in the writing of this book:

Project Muse – https://muse.jhu.edu
Lantern – https://lantern.mediahist.org
Entertainment Industry Magazine Database – https://about.proquest.com/en/products-services/eima
Library of Congress: Chronicling America – https://chroniclingamerica.loc.gov
British Newspaper Archive – www.britishnewspaperarchive.co.uk

Index